This new edition of J accuracy and clarity; new ill making it substantially different from the earlier work of the same name published by Faber and Faber, London, England in1962.

In this richly detailed memoir, **Juliette de Bairacli Levy** – one of the founders of American herbalism – offers us a rare documentary. It is at once an herbal, a travel book, and a compendium of Gypsy lore and Gypsy ways.

Juliette gives us river winds, strange characters in the streets by day, rats scurrying by at night, and legions of cockroaches in the apartments, against whose windows the blossoms of apple and pear trees toss, even in the great city's cement heart.

Part the curtain and enter the hidden world of Gypsies in New York; mysteries await you.

Praise for *A Gypsy in New York*

"Charmingly written, unusual, and captivating. I was sorry when its end came, too quickly to please me."

Helen Siemers

"I am left much wiser concerning that strangest and greatest of the world's cities, New York, my city. In this fascinating book, Gypsy eyes helped me to see New York in all sorts of ways that I formerly had never imagined existed."

Margaret Behrens

In your heart a Gypsy lives; in your fingers a Gypsy dances.

By **Juliette de Bairacli Levy**

from

Ash Tree Publishing

www.ashtreepublishing.com

Common Herbs for Natural Health

A Gypsy in New York

Nature's Children

Spanish Mountain Life

Summer in Galilee

Traveler's Joy

A Gypsy in New York

Juliette de Bairacli Levy

Ash Tree Publishing
Woodstock, NY

Ash Tree Publishing
PO Box 64
Woodstock, NY 12498
845-246-8081

www.wisewomanbookshop.com (to buy our books)
www.ashtreepublishing.com (to learn more about our books and authors)
www.susunweed.com (for more information on herbs)

Publisher's Cataloging in Publication
(Prepared by Quality Books Inc.)

Bairacli-Levy, Juliette de.
A Gypsy in New York / Juliette de Bairacli Levy.
Rev. and updated ed.
p. cm.
Includes index.
LCCN 2005934395
ISBN-13: 978-1-888123-08-1
ISBN-10: 1-888123-08-7

1. Bairacli-Levy, Juliette de. 2. Herbalists–Biography.
3. Materia medica, Vegetable. 4. Medicinal plants.
5. Romanies–New York (State)–New York–Social life and customs. 6. New York (N.Y.)–Description and travel.
I. Title.

RS164.B289 2006 615'.321'092
QBI06-600260

Table of Contents

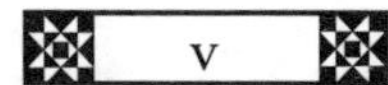

List of Photographs

All photos by Juliette de Bairacli Levy.

Herbal Index

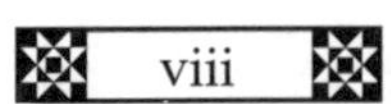

Welcome to New York

New York is the most written-about city in the world. In this book it is seen through unusual eyes, Gypsy eyes, and readers will enjoy new and strange information concerning New York's large Gypsy population, which is still nomadic and hidden from those whom the Gypsies do not accept as their friends.

Author, herbalist, and world traveler, Juliette de Bairacli Levy wanders through New York streets, accompanied by her two young children and her Turkuman Afghan Hounds (for which she is famous). Like the true Romany people, they are more often outdoors than in, and they explore the city in its snow-swept wintertime and its cold early spring.

Juliette describes New York's many wild plants and its wild birds, too. She enjoys the mysterious sight of truckloads of almond blossoms being driven along a Manhattan avenue. And she experiences New York's crime: her money is stolen from her apartment by a dangerous fake window cleaner; she is frightened and chased along the East River walkway by a man and his boxer dog; she witnesses a possible murder in an apartment facing one of her windows; and her beloved amber necklace is bewitched away by a Gypsy friend of deep occult power!

"As a traveler," wrote the poet Stephen Spender in his review in *The Sunday Times* (London), "she makes other recorders of their journeys seem like waterflies skating over the surface of a pond. Her progress across a country seems more antlike, moving from stone to stone, and from stalk to stalk of grass, which is the Gypsy way of looking at things."

La Diamanta Negra: Gypsy dancer and actress of Valencia

Chapter One

New York and Man-a-hat-ta

Like Gypsies, we entered the port of New York in its wintertime, its bleak time. We came with the Atlantic winds – icy-breathed and burdened with snow – and with the winds rising off the great Hudson River, so broad and deep, whose tides flow at one hundred and fifty miles an hour, to join at Albany a system of canals which link New York City with the Great Western Lakes and the Saint Lawrence River. I liked the feel of water and winds around and within New York, and knowing from what places such winds and water came thither. I wondered if sometimes there might drop onto those man-made, confined city streets a plume from a wild goose or wild turkey in flight over that shut-in sky.

Federico Garcia is one of my favorite people, both as person and poet. When he stayed a while in New York, he was inspired to write of its dawn – *la aurora*, that beautiful word – as he saw it:

> "New York's daybreak contains/four columns of mire/and a hurricane of black doves/paddling in putrescent waters."

I saw New York's daybreak differently. I saw gray mists clearing and leaving below valleys of yellowness like the stretches of wild daffodils which I remember with longing from my childhood in England.

A Gypsy in New York

So! New York! Over those misty stretches of yellowness at dawn fly crowds of pigeons or doves – call them either, what you choose – those birds seem as many and as noisy as honeybees emerging from an overturned bee-skep [a hive made of straw]. The New York pigeons are away in search of that day's food. Some receive stale bread or crumbs from compassionate New Yorkers, others fend for themselves amongst garbage; they are clean-natured eaters of cereals only, and decline all other food.

Winter is the season when many Gypsies move into houses in cities all over the world, and they come likewise into New York. The Gypsies are wanting house roofs over their heads during the cold-weather months, and, above all, opportunity to find well-paid work to enable them to amass the wherewithal to travel again, carefree, when the first scents of spring come on the warming air, as the Scottish tinkers say: "When the yellow is on the broom bushes."

A Chinese poet says of that time:

> How fragrant the scent that comes softly with the wind,
> Breaking the traveler's heart in vain
> As he halts his horse, wondering, wandering.

The Gypsies' hearts do not break, the Gypsies go! Now, for American Gypsies, Cadillac cars and upholstered trailers replace the horse-drawn, carved, wooden vans of former days. They follow old and new trails across the Americas of North and South; in Mexico I was to meet, later, American-born Gypsies from New York, mostly traveling in tropical Colima, with its great volcano dominating that beautiful part of the world. Many of the Gypsies in Mexico made their money from sideshows, rather of the Punch and Judy type.

As for "wondering, wandering," I had arrived in New York from southern Spain, with my eight-year-old son, Rafik Nissim, my seven-year-old daughter, Luz España, and an Afghan hound bitch, Cingane. The dog was the greyhound kind which the Gypsies always like to keep, though in this case she was the Afghanistan greyhound breed, not one of the usual hare-chasing "long-tails" of the Gypsy world. In Spain we had stayed in the absolute solitude of the hills of the Malaga territory on a goat farm two hours' donkey-ride away from any village, where the only loud sounds were the pouring of swift streams down rocky courses, and the hundredfold tambourines of shaken goat bells.

Gypsies – equaled only by the nomad Bedouin Arabs – know and love the lonely places of the world. In Spain there are mountain trails which only the Gypsy caravans travel. The contrast of clamorous New York port to the quiet of Malaga hills was extraordinary; but it was also exciting. I have heard many times from traveler friends, people who have lived and worked in many cities, especially writers and artists, that they consider New York to be the most exciting city in the world. I heard one woman passenger on the American Export Lines ship on which we entered the Port of New York telling a woman passenger friend, in her foreign-sounding English, that if you live in New York. "No need go other place, New York got everything!"

I had visited New York fourteen years ago. Then I had come by plane and had been wearing Paris-bought clothes and carried a mere handful of lightweight luggage. Now I had two young children at my side, and all three of us were wearing the sort of odd-looking clothes that long-time travelers tend to wear: rough, hard-wearing materials, wide sleeves for comfort, and many and big pockets to help carry things. I knew that my face had become as weatherworn as that of any old Gypsy woman, although by age I should be considered young. But the heat and the winds of deserts, the cold of mountaintops and the harsh weather of other places where true Gypsy travel takes one, mark the face of travelers as surely as it roughens the stones exposed to it the year around. Not all the lovely herbal lotions that one may make from flowers and leaves, steeped in sunlight and moonlight, can fully protect the skin against changing weather and changing climates.

Also, like Gypsies, I now carried all my possessions with me, as for years I had had no home in which to leave things. So we brought into New York a burdensome weight of my children's collection of toys of the world, to which they were going to add later from New York's fabulous toy shops, and the toy shop of the United Nations, and all their books, the school ones from which I, with much labor, taught them, and their "pleasure" ones; also my own chosen books, and then all the weighty necessities of my two professions, herbalist and writer, including sacks of herbs which I had gathered and dried myself in many countries and used constantly, volumes of notes for books on herbs, human and veterinary, and notes on our travel. I intended to write these books one day, but meanwhile carried them from country to country, still unwritten! And then cameras and artist's materials, and a heavy collection of ancient stones and pots which my children and I had dug out of their hiding places in Europe, Mexico, and Israel. Some had gone into museums; others we could not bear to part with. Our luggage was now a collection of big wicker traveling basket-trunks, made by Gypsies from such places as Poland and Spain, and also peasant-made from that lovely island of Madeira, rightly famed for its baskets.

There was reason in such choice of luggage: the Gypsies store their possessions in sacks from the same motives. When clothing has to remain packed for months, it needs ventilation to prevent mustiness and discoloration. In the primitive places where we have stayed, from Gypsy tents to old water-mills, and even ruins, our trunks are usually our only furniture, both for storing things and for sitting on. As I write this, we are living far from New York, in an old Greek church by the Sea of Galilee, in Israel. Our cell-like room is furnished with two beds and one table only, therefore our luggage is again in use for storage and for seating! And we will probably be living in this room for three months.

The sky of New York held my attention. In winter it seems to be a very high sky: artists have commented on this. Its color, when the sun is not shining, is usually ashen, and against that pale color, the famous heaven-reaching, fantastic, often monolithic, buildings of Manhattan look darkly gray. Because Manhattan is such a narrow stretch of land – it is described as being not unlike a fish in shape – the New York builders, once they had built on every possible inch of the limited ground space, and still the demand for offices and apartments increased, had to build upwards towards the clouds; thus their descriptive name: "skyscrapers."

All who come to New York and look upon its crowding buildings, more pressed together and far more towering than any buildings anywhere else on earth, cannot help but think back to the time when, only a few hundred years ago, the only dwellings on that now crowded area of Manhattan were a few scattered lodges of the peaceful Canarsie Indians. It was said to have been a place of wild roses and brambles which yielded wonderful blackberries. Perhaps it was the fragrance of those Manhattan wild roses which made the Indians name that land, which the surrounding rivers make an island, *Man-a-hat-ta*, which means in their beautiful language "Heavenly Land." The official flower of New York State, aptly, is the wild rose.

As a botanist, I know that two wild American plants are named after New York, the New York aster and New York fern. The state has flower festivals: Every year an Apple Blossom Festival is held at Rochester, and later a Lilac Festival elsewhere.

New York State's motto is equally apt: *Excelsior*, "Ever Upward." Looking around at the Manhattan skyline reaching its climax in the Empire State Building, which pierces the sky like a giant's hypodermic syringe, one wonders if the motto was chosen with Manhattan in mind.

Now the roses and blackberry bushes are found only in the parks, and there is no heavenly fragrance. Nostril-pricking fumes of petrol from the exhaust pipes of vehicles of every kind which teem in every street in the city, belching fumes from the numerous factories which surround New York City and poison the city's heart, all afflict one's nose and lungs. Like the Gypsies, I am always conscious of the "poisoned air of cities," throughout my time in New York, and later, in Los Angeles, where I suffered worst of all.

The waterfront of New York, stretching as far as one's eyes can see ahead, seems enormous, and there are, indeed, about seven hundred miles of it. Many nostalgic seamen's songs have been written about it. It faces numerous small islands, the most famous and romantic of these islands being that on which stands the Liberty statue. All ships' passengers approaching New York keep a lookout for the towering Statue of Liberty, that splendid woman of copper standing on a small, water-splashed piece of land in New York harbor. Sea mists and salty winds blown inland from the Atlantic have grayed and greened the copper figure and made her more beautiful: she is a perching place for seagulls and other sea birds, and sometimes, oh! wonderful! wild geese.

Although she is of Amazon type and her face is stern, for she must protect her torch of Liberty from being blown out by any oppressing forces, the words inscribed at her feet are tender enough. I knew that they had been composed for the statue by a young Jewish woman, Emma Lazarus. My father, when I was a girl, had once given me a small volume of her poems. I had been impressed then by the promise of the Golden Door. But I have ceased to look for Golden Doors into anywhere, for I have come to believe that life is really more fun on the other side, among the ragged Bohemians. I wanted to know the complete words of the inscribed verse on the Statue of Liberty as our ship sailed past. I wanted to tell them to my children as they stood at my side marveling at New York harbor. Therefore it was strange to me that of the twelve Americans around me on the ship whom I asked – one of them a schoolmistress and most of them New Yorkers – not one of them could tell me the words! Here they are, beautiful in their promise to all homeless wanderers [from "The New Colossus" by Emma Lazarus]:

> "Give me your tired, your poor,
> Your huddled masses yearning to breathe free,
> The wretched refuse of your teeming shore.
> Send these, the homeless, tempest-tost to me,
> I lift my lamp beside the golden door!"

The immense statue was presented by France to America, in admiration and friendship, symbolic of the liberty and freedom enjoyed by all citizens of America under a free government, elected freely by the people for the people. A symbol of Liberty enlightening the world.

Nowadays "the wretched [human] refuse" find America a difficult country to enter. The official question-forms to be completed, and the guarantees to be made, would baffle most modern wandering Gypsies wishing to enter as immigrants. My children and I came only as visitors to America, and that was difficult enough. Then, on arrival, there was talk of detaining us on Ellis Island because of my absolute refusal to have my children and dog vaccinated.

As an herbalist I keep my children and animals – dogs and goats – all safe and healthy on the medicines of the Bible: the herbs and the grasses. I fear no disease, and so far, with the exception of typhus in Spain years ago, I have not had to pay out one cent to any doctor other than for an occasional certificate of good health needed as we travel from country to country. Herbal medicine is also Native American medicine, well known to those who occupied the New York State region before the coming of the Dutch: the Great Peaceful Nations of the Iroquois Confederacy. These farmers, hunters, and fishermen were some of the largest and most powerful of the North American Indian nations.

Close to the island of the Statue of Liberty is Ellis Island, the gateway into New York that is also a detention and deportation center of the United States Immigration Service. For two centuries New York itself has been an Eldorado to pressing crowds of immigrants and exiles from Europe, and among those human masses, many thousands of Serbian and Balkan Gypsies entered at the time of World War I.

The Jewish population of New York City is enormous: at times, as high as 30 percent of the population [in 2002, 12 percent were Jewish]. In the Lower East Side thousands of Jews occupy whole streets, but there is no ghetto there or anywhere in America. The American Jewish people are a free and prosperous minority, and their genius has created many of New York's most famous and most beautiful stores. Christopher Columbus's voyage to the New World was supposed to have been financed largely by Portuguese Jews. At the time of Columbus's voyage, King Ferdinand had already turned his jealous eyes upon the flourishing Jews of Spain, and the Spanish and Portuguese Jews anxiously hoped that that great navigator, perhaps of their own race, as some historians have decided, would find them a new country to which they could flee from the commencing agony of the Spanish Inquisition.

And that was exactly what came to be, although not as refugees from the Spanish persecutors; that was too early, the Jews of Spain leaving then for Holland, Yugoslavia, Greece, Turkey, and thereabouts. My own family on my father's side left Toledo for Smyrna in Turkey, and on my mother's side they went from Barcelona to Tetuan in Spanish Morocco and to Marrakesh; and they still bear names such as Barchelon and Maratchi.

It was the Jews of Russia and Poland who swarmed to the New World to escape the more recent *pogroms* of those lands, and yet later on, the German, Polish, Hungarian, and other Jews from Hitler's Nazi-occupied countries found refuge in America from the worst *pogroms* of their history: refuge from unspeakable mass death in gas chambers or in execution pits. That is why the European Jews predominate in America and the Sephardic – Spanish and Portuguese – Jews are still only a small percentage in comparison.

No one who has ever embarked at New York port can fail to agree that it is among the most beautiful, largest, and best of all the great ports of the world. It is claimed that New York harbor could easily contain any six of the world's largest ports.

Other than the birch-bark canoes of the original Indian inhabitants, the small ship, Half Moon, sailed by the European Henry Hudson, was the first to travel, in 1609, the majestic river that leads to Manhattan Island. The river bears the explorer's name, the Hudson, and so does one of New York's hotels, the Henry Hudson, where I was to attend the annual dog show of the American Afghan Hound Association.

The part-English explorer, Hudson, was in the employ of the Dutch East India Company. It was the Dutch who first settled Manhattan and the surrounding areas and called their settlement New Amsterdam. Here is a legend, and it is true! that Peter Minuit, a governor of the Dutch trading company, purchased Manhattan Island from "the wild men" for $24 worth of baubles and a small amount of fancy cloth. In land value alone, it is worth untold millions of dollars only a few hundred years later, and the population has grown from a handful of Indians to millions of

Three dancing girls of La Faraona, Sacromonte, Granada

people who have come from all over the world to settle and trade there.

I was coming to "trade" in books. A number of American publishers had written to my English publishers, Faber and Faber, concerning their interest in a book that I had written about Galilee of the Holy Land, legends and true travel tales (*Summer in Galilee*, now published by Ash Tree Publishing). With the help of a New York literary agent, Paul Reynolds, American publication of that book, and several of my earlier ones, was envisaged. So now I, too, had come to the Golden Door, rather old and tired and much traveled.

Before I left Granada, in Spain, my Gypsy friend, the great dancer La Faraona (one of the Gypsy priestesses of the famed mountain caves dancing-places of Sacro Monte), had taken my hand unasked and had begun reading it! I had never seen her hand reading before, and she seemed in a trance, as she pressed her powerful dancer's leg against mine. She prophesied great success in America.

I was not to find it! Moderate success in my work, but the making of many American friends and friendships that I know will endure my life through. Success may come later! Faraona had seemed so sure. And indeed, she is always questioning any friends of mine who had come from America to Spain, asking them: Had I made my fortune? Faraona is dead now. Her remarkable face is deeply etched on my mind. I miss her. We will meet again likely in the spirit world of the dead. Some friendships are everlasting.

Safely in through the Golden Door, past the Customs officials, who I feared might seize my harmless herbs if they found them, perhaps believing them to be some form of the forbidden marijuana – and they had not at all liked the look of luggage in the form of big, travel-battered baskets – I was able to gaze about me, with quieter eyes, at the New York scene. Taking one's eyes away from the pleasing, natural waters of the great river on which our ship still rode, I was pleased to see natural-looking rocks on one side of the harbor, and here and there clumps of trees or a solitary tree, leafless now in the month of December. All else around looked artificial, so much a show of man's cleverness that, although as I came to know Manhattan well, and the rest of New York a little, and to find much beauty after all, I was, at that moment, regretting the lack of the American Indians in their peaceful setting among the wild roses and the bramble thickets! In England, those plants remain in leaf, green turning to gold, well into January. Now, leafless and stony gray, the inimical-seeming world stretched around me filled with a noise of moving vehicles that was incredible in its volume and diversity, and not pleasing at all.

I know that it is claimed that New York city has more trees than buildings or people, and city officials are trying to keep it that way. But the great old elms of Washington Square and other places in the city, are stricken with disease and falling. Can trees really live and flourish in poisoned, polluted air, drinking dirty water streaked with petrol from the teeming motor vehicles?

The pear tree of New York's good and romantic first Governor, Peter Stuyvesant, survived through nearly three centuries, but had to be cut down recently. Legend tells us that Stuyvesant used one of his pear-tree boughs for a new peg leg, when he had worn down the first one through his habit of stamping with it upon the ground to emphasize his orders. I regretted that I was not to see what must have been New York's most famous tree. And a pear tree, even an ordinary, non-famous one, is always a lovely thing in its blossom-time. That must have looked good, the white fleeces of pear blossom, wind-tossed against the surrounding monotonous gray of the city buildings. And apple blossom also, rose-tinted on the white. Those sweet trees' blossoms are truly a refreshment to the nostrils and the soul.

New York State has fame for its apple orchards, some of which are truly vast. But those apple orchards have not given New York its strange and endearing name: "The Big Apple."

An American schoolgirl, Emma Palmer, had the intelligence to make use of the New York free information service, which will answer queries concerning New York, so we could learn about the Big Apple. It is associated with jazz players, who call a job "an apple." A gig or job in New York is a big apple. Later, New York itself came to be called "The Big Apple." There are porcelain cups for sale in New York shops with a big red apple on them and the two words "New York." Yet, surprisingly, few people know how the apple and New York came to be associated. Merely ask your New York friends to confirm this!

Whenever I hear about unusual events in world weather patterns, losses of forest, and other strange phenomena afflicting the world, such as the reports that famed ancient monuments – like the pyramids of Egypt and the Acropolis of Greece – are crumbling, I am always possessed by worrying thoughts as to the far-reaching and as yet incalculable effects of atomic bomb test explosions. More than the scientists, the simple peasants of the world greatly fear them. I was surprised when first I learned that the peasants interest themselves in the atomic explosions, but they certainly do. And the Gypsies of the world, who are still greatly gifted with the powers of prophecy, warn frequently against the experiments, which they say bring with them a "charnel smell" to the earth and its waters.

I have been told about Jacob Joshua Levison, Chief Forester for the City of New York, who as a boy had come from Latvia to the slums of Manhattan's Lower East Side. Wanting the trees that he must have known in his early childhood in Latvia, he became one of the greatest crusaders for conservation of America's trees and forests. He was associated with places where trees survive – the Cloisters, and the gardens of the Metropolitan Museum of Art and of Tudor City – which saved New York from becoming an ugly city. It was this tree- and plant-loving man who created one of the largest and most original of the roof gardens of Manhattan, covering almost two acres, and remarkably being only six feet above the level of the street and built over a garage roof, of a 300-car capacity. This man said that it was "the sordidness of a treeless existence that caused me to choose forestry over other vocations. Then, as now, the aesthetic aspects of trees appealed to me as much as the practical ones."

As soon as my children got out into the New York streets they noticed the iron or wooden railings around the trees, and "No Climbing" notices by many of the surviving rocks in the public parks.

"What are we to climb?" they asked me in dismay. "No trees! No rocks!"

"You'll find plenty of climbing in New York buildings!" I assured them. "No need to use the elevators, we have legs to carry us up and down places, as you know!"

The sun came out above the towering rooftops of Manhattan. Then the harbor sky was no longer ashen; daffodil streaks appeared there, and golden sun-rays like the tall yellow candles I have seen the Baltic Gypsies carrying to the shrine of the world's only Gypsy saint, the Black Virgin, Sainte Sara, who has domain over her underground chapel, beneath the ancient church of Les Saintes Maries de la Mer, in the French Camargue, Provence.

The sun over New York! When later I came to know artists in New York, they told me that, in wintertime, nowhere in Europe, not even in southern Spain famous for its light, is there to be found more sun and light than along the open places of New York, by its waterfront and its parks.

But all the time I was in New York the sun was associated with one of my greatest frustrations: for there is nowhere to sunbathe! Every grimy rooftop, every patch of parkland, seemed overlooked. I am, with all my being, a sun and fire worshiper. And I do not mean the artificial fire or light from electric sunlamps or fire stoves or gas fires! I mean the powerful, naked sun, and the flames from true Gypsy fires of piled wood or turf, or next best, from rich chunks of coal. When one sunbathes and firebathes, one never feels cold. In the bitterest of New York subzero [Farenheit] weather, I was always warm; I never once wore a topcoat. Because immediately before coming to America, I had been fed for three years by the sun of Spanish Andalusia and later of Mexico, living always in primitive places where it was possible to sunbathe completely.

Whenever the sun was shining I envied the New York pigeons. Sun-seekers, like all the family of the doves, they flitted from sunlit ledge to sunlit ledge of the New York buildings, and the golden light gilded their plumage, which has the colors and the shimmer of iris flowers. In Washington Square I found the pigeons more at home, as if in their original woodland setting, for there in the Square they had found tree hollows for nesting places, and on sunny mornings, even in the winter months, they made their soothing pigeon sounds, which were a strange but pleasing addition to the surrounding noise of Manhattan.

The modern steam heating of New York, Chicago, and other towns in North America that experience cold winters is considered an essential of civilized life. Yet most foreign visitors to New York complain about the stifling heat of New York apartments, stores, and restaurants. I was never able to accept, enjoy, or understand that unbearable, airless heating; it seemed to me to be the best formula for catching a true New York feverish cold, from which most of my friends were suffering at one time or another whenever I was in that city. To go out from such unnatural heat to the cold of often ten degrees below zero in the streets!

Those over-hot New York buildings made me often feel that I was being slowly steamed alive, like a crab in this horrible recipe, which a beer firm was advertising under the headline: "From Chesapeake Bay, land of pleasant living." Here it is:

> Use a steampot that has an elevated platform. For every dozen crabs used, put into the steamer one cup of beer, one cup of vinegar, and enough water to cover.
>
> Place live, soft crabs that have just shed their shells on platform in layers, sprinkle seasoning (salt, pepper, mustard, paprika, cayenne) between the layers of crabs. Steam (do not boil) for about twenty minutes, until crabs are a fiery red and ready to eat.

Shameful. However, despite the present-day world being meaner and crueler to animals than ever before, many crabs and lobsters are now first stabbed through the back before being steamed.

As if the slow steaming alive were not agony enough, the additional sprinkling of burning spices pricks the eyes and other parts of the live creatures piled upon one another. And crabs are wise and clever. I came to know very well the land crabs of tropical Mexico and also the sweetwater crabs of the Sea of Galilee. No wonder that I bring up my two children to be vegetarians and hope they will stay that way. I read out the crab recipe to them as a reminder.

The Gypsies are some of the New York winter visitors who complain most about steam heating and are nostalgic for their big outdoor fires. Like migratory birds, hundreds, perhaps thousands, of Gypsies enter New York for the winter season, congregating especially in and around Manhattan and Brooklyn. They come for the profitable fortune-telling earnings of their women, and the odd metal-repairing piecework and cloth-trade dealing of their men. Many of the Gypsy lads work profitably as bootblacks.

They come also in troupes as dancers and singers, and the Hungarians among them provide violin music in restaurants and cafes. Many of them have been living outdoors in desert parts of California or in North America's numerous forests, for even the American Gypsy, the most "civilized" of their race, remains nomad at heart: now they come to stifle in the city. The American Gypsy mostly truck-travels today, although many of the fortune-telling families use expensive Cadillac cars and well-equipped trailers when on the roads. Indeed, Cadillacs are the most typical of the many cars that the American Gypsies drive.

Countless New York Gypsies have commiserated with me concerning the unpleasantness of life in steam-heated apartments. They stifle in the overheating, but when windows are opened the street dirt blows in upon them. If they turn off all the heating they freeze with the damp cold of shut-in house-places where the sunlight never enters. Gypsies in New York nearly always rent ground-floor rooms, because not only do they like to see the road, their beloved *drom*, around them, but it is also better for business. However, today many Gypsies have to be satisfied with first-floor apartments. There they are still close enough to their *drom* for life to be bearable. One seldom finds Gypsies living higher up than the first floor.

And the Gypsies of New York, where are they? One of the first thoughts that occupy my mind when entering any new city is "Will there be Gypsies? And, where will I find them?" One is told, ask the police! They always keep track of the Gypsies! But do they keep track? I think they are unable to do so still; for it is rightly said of the New York Gypsies that no one knows how many there are in the city because they are nomads. They move from borough to borough and neighborhood to neighborhood, when they are not traveling farther afield from city to city or from state to state. Then, more persistently than any other race, the

Gypsies keep two or more names; constant enmity with soldiers and police has driven them to this. So the Gypsies have two names, a Romany family one and a "civilized" one in keeping with the land in which they settle or travel most. This second name they use for school (if their children ever attend one), business, and the police. The Gypsies themselves have told me that their population in New York is a shifting one of around 3,000 in the wintertime, but far less in the spring and summer. They reckoned that [in the 1960s] in Los Angeles they were about 7,000 strong.

I get to know the Gypsies of every town that I visit, because I am sure of finding among them loyal friendship and interesting companionship and true amusement, song, music, dance, magic, all of these and more; love, sometimes.

In any Spanish or Turkish or Balkan town one is almost sure to find a Gypsy quarter, also in many French towns; but New York has no Gypsy quarter nowadays, although I believe there was one once. I had no intention of asking the police to help me to find my friends! The only American guidebook that I ever saw which mentioned the Gypsies said there was a Gypsy quarter in New York in the neighborhood of the Essex Street market.

The book went on to say that around Broome Street, close by the market, there are many dark-complexioned people living in ground-floor places such as long-abandoned warehouses, or tenting out in backyards. These families are especially numerous along Attorney Street, where almost every ground-floor room is occupied by them. As their doors are nearly always open, it was easy to look inside and see the strangely "foreign" dwelling places of hanging curtains dividing the rooms into smaller portions, where family lived along with other families. Mattress beds or rag-littered floors, very little furniture, and charcoal brazier fires in wintertime; and above all, flocks of dark-faced children with flashing smiles and teeth of pearls, the only begging children in that poor-class neighborhood, who dart out from almost every home, pleading, "Gimme a nickel, kind lady, kind genilman, gimme a dime" – these are the proofs. "These are the Gypsies," the guidebook said.

And the book description is true enough of the *kair* (house) Gypsies of New York. For no matter how prosperous the fortune-telling Gypsies are, they nearly always choose to sleep behind their place or in their place, after the clients have gone away. They prefer bedrolls on the floor, thin, mattress-type things, which they will roll up and store away during the daytime. And the same house-living plan

Tent-dwelling Gypsies; Valencia, Spain

applies also to the other American Gypsies, whether they are the fortune-tellers or not. Some even erect tents inside the stores, and burn wood chips inside old tins, and that way fire worship as usual, although to a very limited extent!

I went to the Essex Street neighborhood in search of the Gypsies soon after my arrival in New York, but although I found there people from almost all lands, including many of the old-fashioned Yiddish-speaking types of black-clad European Jews, and many Puerto Ricans in gaudy clothes, there were no Gypsies to be seen. I patiently searched every street in the neighborhood and made inquiries in many shops. That way, from the shopkeepers, I did find that Gypsies had lived there once, but only as recently as a year ago their places had all been condemned and the tenements had been pulled down. Now big new apartment houses stood ready completed where the Gypsy tents had once been in the open yards, and more big modern buildings were being erected. Indeed, that typical noise of New York – building construction – could be heard on all sides: that hammering of steel girders, the whirring of the concrete mixers, and the knock of bricks falling or being laid into place. One Jewish grocer said he did remember the Gypsy families of Attorney Street, "Nice people, very handsome. They seemed to live mostly on bread and bars of chocolate. Did not use electric lights, liked to burn candles."

I thought of the Gypsies that New York friends had described to me. Jean Goldfarb remembered when Gypsy families used to encamp at Jamaica, by Long Island. In her childhood there, a copse of trees was still standing, and the Gypsies would come and stay there, bringing with them their van-houses of beautifully carved wood, pulled along by fine and mettlesome horses, greyhounds running at their sides. They would light fires and sit around them. The local children used to hurry from school to the Gypsy encampment and would be allowed to look inside the wagons and see the babies in wooden-box cradles. The schoolchildren were asked by the Gypsies to bring them a little boxwood kindling for their fires, and roots – potatoes, carrots, turnips – or stale bread leftovers, in return for the privilege of being allowed to see inside the Gypsy wagons, to sit on the horses' backs, to play with the greyhound puppies, and so forth.

Jean remembered very well that the Gypsy people, not their animals, had a peculiar smell about them, "like goats." The New York schoolchildren found that very exciting; people who really smelled like goats and who also spoke a language to each other that was quite unlike any of the many foreign jargons commonly heard in the New York streets. Then further, they were a people who would suddenly strike up a wild singing or dancing for seemingly no other reason than that they wished to sing and dance, while they were leading in their horses or chopping wood for their fires. And sometimes they would pick up one of their brown babies and toss the child from one person to another across the leaping fire flames, to the astonishment of the New York children watching, and the unmistakable pleasure of the tossed little Gypsy.

Carol Cohen remembered a pre-funeral ceremony for a Gypsy queen, in New York, on Henry Street. Like Jean Goldfarb, Carol was a child then. It was a ground-floor room, made brilliant and dramatic with candles burning in the daytime and heaped flowers of all colors. Teeming Gypsy mourners, mostly black-clad, filled the room. A frightened, yet enchanted, party of little New York schoolgirls determinedly pushed their way into the room until they had a sufficient viewing place of the dead Gypsy queen. The children never let go their hold of each other's hands, as they had agreed before entering. Their great fear had been the Gypsy reputation of being child-stealers, and they had decided that the Gypsies could not take them all joined together in a heavy, fleshy chain of eight little girls!

The queen had been laid out on a cloth-draped table, her head upon an embroidered pillow, a big candle at her feet, another at her head. Smaller candles on all sides. But most impressive had been the jewelry piled upon her and flashing in the candlelight. Jewels hanging from the woman's withered ears, around her scraggy neck and burdening her thin arms. Jewels that scintillated like stars and glowed like fires. The dazzled Carol Cohen had asked of one of the Gypsies standing at the side of the old queen:

"Will she take all that with her into her grave?"

No reply had been spoken by the Gypsy mourner, only such a malignant look of scorn and hate directed upon the inquiring non-Gypsy that the little girls, still holding hands, decided in quick consultation that they had seen enough, and it was time to go!

Although I searched carefully, I did not find any Gypsies in New York during my entire first month there. The only Gypsies that I saw were embroidered on a medieval tapestry in French's famous antique shop on Madison Avenue. I was offering a Chinese butterfly silk shawl of mine for sale there, and I was invited to look over the many floors of that wonderful, treasure-packed place. There I came upon the Gypsies on the tapestry. I was told that it was called "The Birthday of the Empress." It showed the rich being entertained by a family of traveling Gypsies who were reading the hands of the Empress and her party.

I myself learned fortune-telling from an old Algerian Gypsy, a Madame Caulas of the family Heredia, whom I met in the Rue de la Corderie in the Gypsy quarter of Marseilles. A strange place of shacks, where the riffraff of the town lived along with the Gypsies, who were mostly of the fortune-telling, basket-making, dancer, and street-singer class. Madame Caulas was considered to be an expert in three forms of fortune telling: hand reading, sand reading, and reading the mysterious Tarot cards of the Bohemians.

I did not find it difficult to learn hand reading the Gypsy way, as taught by Madame Caulas. Perhaps the old woman had foretold rightly that I had the Gypsy gift of *dukkeripen*, (reading, magic reading). Soon the Gypsies of many lands, including America and Mexico, were asking me to read their hands! The "deep reading," they call it.

"That," said American writer friend Michael Kuh, "is a subject for a cartoon! An English university-educated young woman, reared in a strict English school [in my case it was an old Welsh castle converted into a school for the daughters of rich English and Welsh gentry] even though her blood is Turkish, reading the hands of the hard-baked professional fortune-telling Gypsies of New York!"

A friend, Roy Nicholls, told me about a Gypsy fortune-telling cartoon he saw: Marked "Lexington Avenue," it showed a street window, with a scarf-draped Gypsy woman's head peering out. Alongside was a big notice, which read: "Psychoanalysis $1, palm-reading $2."

I did not meet with any Gypsies in New York until well into the New Year, when I came to know many families of them, in Manhattan.

Gypsies of Sacromonte; the author, center in dark blouse.

Chapter Two

Urban Oddities

Two wide windows of a first floor apartment on the corner of 78th Street of Manhattan's Second Avenue gave an interesting impression of New York City life. There was never a lull in the procession of traffic of all kinds that went down the broad, one-way street. When the usual assortment of teeming taxis, buses, commercial vans, and private cars had slackened off, and the midnight hour came and went, then the heavy truck traffic took over in the early dawn hours when the winter mornings were cold-possessed and very still, or ranting with the incoming sea winds that brought snow and sleet to the sleeping city.

The big trucks passing below my windows bore the names of almost every state in America, from the Empire State of New York itself to such distant places as Texas, Arizona, California, Washington and Oregon.

An old New York church on the East Side, the Shrine of the Sea, supplied special prayer tracts for truck drivers as well as for seamen and other travelers. And as I watched the trucks go by at dawn, skidding along the streets, which were often ice-bound, and thought of the great distances ahead of most of them, I felt that the drivers certainly needed special prayers to help them safely to their destinations.

What a noise the full daytime traffic of New York made all the time that I lived within close sound of it. One's ears were assaulted, and yet it was only the background refrain to the other common sounds of the city: the screaming sirens of the ambulances, fire engines, and police cars, and the din of road menders and house builders. (An old house adjoining the one in which I was staying was being knocked down and rebuilt.)

Once there had been an overhead railway across Second Avenue, but the subway and the wonderful and colossal modern bridges have changed much of the face of old New York. I think that more than any other city I have known, the face of New York is the most changeable. The profile remains fairly constant, but, for the rest, one never knows on each return visit what one will find gone and what new.

The television tower on top of the Empire State Building on Fifth Avenue was new, taking that building almost one and a half thousand feet up into the sky. At night the fiery finger of its red light summit seems to press into the region of the dim stars.

Also new, and now important on the Manhattan skyline, is the clean-cut, beautiful, many-windowed building of the United Nations in its riverside setting.

In Greenwich Village many fine old houses have been torn down in recent years and been replaced by mammoth, characterless blocks of apartments renting at very high prices, far beyond the purse of the average Bohemian of the Village. Many of these new buildings in the Village overlook the fountain of Washington Square, in which the "Improper Bohemian" women of that area used to celebrate various important village events, including May Day, by taking a nude dip.

On my recent visit to Washington Square there was no water to be seen in its fountain, only a dry, stony circle smattered with pigeons' droppings. Loving, as I do, cold, splashing water, I might have been tempted to take a dip there myself if there had been water in the fountain!

As I was not writing a book while in New York but merely collecting material for one, my children and I were again able to lead the life of wandering Gypsies, with hound at side, out on "the road" in all weathers and at all hours. For most of our time there it was winter: but bad weather does not keep Gypsies in houses!

I like wintertime in New York, with the threat of snow – brought citywards on the winds from sea and river – always present in the air. The American Indians called these "Winds of the White Deer." Also, they called the heavy rainstorms of the winter "Male Rain," while the warmer and more gentle showers of the spring were "Female Rain."

Before such winter rainstorms the sky was often like thick black treacle. I was always thankful for the cleansing downpours of the winter storms, for New York City, except in the vicinity of Central Park and the center parts of Fifth Avenue and Park Avenue, and several of the other near avenues, is not a clean place. One has only to watch new snowfall turn from its dazzling white to gray-black within a few hours to realize the amount of dirt that is blowing everywhere. The air in the New York subway, caught in a shaft of light filtering through, is an unpleasant sight to see with its suspended filth.

It is said of many New York pavements that "filth shoves against filth." That is certainly true of many of the neighborhoods in which we walked. On those sidewalks of the Bowery, the Bronx, Harlem, and many reaches of First, Second, Third, and others of the avenues, including Avenue of the Americas, away in the Village, it was difficult to avoid treading on dog and cat excreta, soiled papers, straw, slivers of wood, mucus from unclean mouths, glass from broken bottles, and so on.

And all the while the surrounding factories of New York blew their belches of poison smoke upon us and all the other people walking in the streets, and grimed the wilting trees that totter on their filth-nourished roots, protected by grime-painted palisades from the acid urine of the many city dogs.

Refuse clearance seems one of the problems of New York. There are bins in the streets outside the apartment houses, and it is a finable offense to deposit litter in the roads or parks; and all refuse bins must have lids put over them. Only in New York, such a region of gusty winds, lids are often blown off. And the bins are often too crammed with litter to carry a lid. So, on sidewalk and street, the wind-lifted, typical New York litter of paper, empty food and cigarette wrappers, cartons and empty small food cans will perform a strange Irish jig, round and round, wind-whipped into a mad dance.

Dead dogs and cats are also put into the New York refuse bins. I remember one night when walking down First Avenue, my children and I were startled at seeing the head of a large white cat staring out at us forbiddingly, with a lid across its neck. I soon saw that it was dead and would no longer prowl the gray land of concrete that must have been its former unattractive territory.

When a poodle puppy of a friend died, he was put out into a refuse bin. That puppy had been a typical unhealthy product of city life. He had been raised from the time he was weaned on a lifeless diet of pasteurized milk, cooked meat out of cans, and fancy biscuits out of packets. This city poodle had almost never had sunlight on its body, nor had he been able to get the raw flesh diet and medicinal grasses such as had once been available for the stalwart and disease-free dogs that companioned the American Indians. A distemper vaccination shot killed that poodle puppy within three days. My children had come to know the small black dog. They had given it a Christmas present of a toy mouse of gray velvet that squeaked when pressed. Weeping, the two children had rescued the poodle from the bin and brought it to me, for "a kinder grave under a tree." Such a grave we had once made for a cat of ours that had been poisoned.

I decided that the only possible grave available to us in Manhattan would be a watery one: the East River. I promised my children that we could made a small boat from one of our Spanish Gypsy baskets (at quite a sacrifice for me, as I valued everyone of my many baskets), put the dead puppy inside, and send it away down the river. I felt sure that dead things should not be put *into* the river, although the bodies of gangsters killed in gang fights are said to show up now and then in that very river. Nevertheless, I prepared the basket, put the toy mouse in along with the poodle for companionship, Gypsy-like. And then, with much difficulty, launched the basket-boat on its journey. I remember the seagulls in a wailing company overhead, and yet farther up in the sky, those typical clouds of the East River in winter months, which resemble a flock of gray-white sheep huddled together, dispersed by the strong winds, only to come together in their flocks again.

There is much refuse too bulky to go into the bins and so put out in the New York streets. One can see anything there as one walks by. The refuse-collecting vans go by nightly – along Second Avenue, their hour is midnight – but sometimes they leave items of rubbish for weeks, as happened with an old mattress that came into the street a few blocks away from where we lived; it appeared as if it would crawl away with the bedbugs that must live in such a stained, rent, and horrible-looking thing! There were old chairs put out into the gutter, chairs of broken cane, others of armchair type, with the stuffing hanging out. Once we were amused to see at midday down 78th Street, off First

Avenue, a truly ragged tramp, sitting in a thrown-out armchair in the gutter, and there eating his luncheon, splendidly, with a can of beer for complete refreshment. There was cast out broken crockery, broken wooden toilet seats, old corsets, one battered guitar in such a state it looked as if it must have been used to club somebody, old gramophone records, broken toys, and often umbrellas that were blown inside-out, typical in New York's gusty winter weather.

Strangely, despite the usually crowded pavements, many New Yorkers use umbrellas in rainy weather. Then, New York's winds catch them, and the material by the metal spokes is quickly torn. One windy morning my children and I counted nearly a dozen abandoned umbrellas standing upright in Manhattan street-corner bins.

Litter that I liked to see, and which was typical of New York, was discarded Christmas trees and boughs. Nowhere is Christmas celebrated more ardently or romantically than in New York. Thousands of Christmas trees go up into the apartment houses and at the ending of the Christmas festival, they come down again into the streets. There they are piled, often for days, green and natural looking on the stretching miles of monotonous concrete. Many of the trees were still entangled with their adornments of silver streamers and tinsel, which glittered like stardust when street and shop-window lamps shone down upon them. Some of the trees also still carried their bright Stars of Bethlehem. When it snowed on the piled tree litter, all became extra beautiful; and when it rained, one could smell resin, and walk again in

memory through lonely pine forests where there were wild deer and quiet-winged owls. The New York animals, dogs and cats, all loved the green, rustling litter, the few cats allowed there played at jungle games, and the dogs trampled on the springy places and, sadly, urinated there also.

Snow fell frequently during our winters in New York. As everywhere in the world where there is snowfall, it came down over the city in its quiet and mysterious way, silent as the white hawthorn blossom of springtime that tumbles from laden boughs to pile around the roots of the thorn bushes. And, as fallen blossom petals do rapidly become discolored, so likewise the city snow. To enjoy snow in its pure white beauty when in New York City, one seemingly had to go to the top of the Empire State Building or to some lofty, private penthouse, where it would remain for days, unsmutched and unearthly.

We enjoyed unspoiled and truly virgin snow in country parts of New York State. Away on Long Island, at Sands Point, where there are marshes that wild duck and geese still frequent, and woods where rabbits, pheasants, and woodcock etch their tracks over the snow, my children enjoyed the New York winter pleasures of tobogganing, making giant snowmen, and watching the skilled skaters flying like dark birds over frozen waterways. Farther afield in the neighbor states of Connecticut and New Jersey, we saw skiing, and again human adults and children became birdlike as they skimmed over the snow-covered foothills. I could never tire of the snow, although often when visiting the country places we were snowbound for days. During our second New York winter the snowfall was breaking records, and it lay on the ground either newly fallen or as frozen heaps almost continuously from early December until mid-February, when we left America for the Sea of Galilee.

Snow clearance was always a problem in New York City, probably because of the vast and crowded area to be cleared, the difficulty of obtaining outdoor manual labor, and the high wages that such commanded. I remember young boys, equipped merely with shovels, asking ten dollars for clearing driveways of snow on Long Island, work requiring an hour or less, and getting that price.

Around Washington Square, I saw motor-driven hand plows and brushes in use for snow clearance, but elsewhere, except for half-hearted shoveling by truck crews, who cleaned the roads but left the paved sidewalks untouched, the snow was allowed to stay for days, until it melted away into yellow-gray rivers. I remember our first Christmas shopping in New York was done while pushing through ankle-deep snow sludge, even on Fifth Avenue, where the rich were soiling and spoiling their elegant shoes and stockings. With the big holiday crowds in the city, its 11,500 taxis were all taken, and there were not nearly enough to serve the people waiting to use them.

In most parts of the city, people were made responsible for cleaning away the snow from their own steps and portion of sidewalk. If they failed to do this and any pedestrian slipped there and was injured, they were liable for the medical expenses. Therefore, with that unpleasant thought in mind, if not for any other reason, everyone who possessed property in the city was out with snow scrapers, shovels, and brushes, or were paying others to clean up for them, after every snowfall. As I always like any reason to be out in the fresh air and also enjoy any kind of manual labor, I was happy to help with the snow clearance from my friend Dana Miller's place, above which was the good apartment that she had let me have rent-free for as long as I cared to enjoy it.

The two wide front windows of our apartment overlooked Second Avenue, at 78th Street. Our back windows in a long, adjoining room, overlooked the corner where Second Avenue joined 78th Street. Books about cities have been written from observations made from a window. I remember such titles as "A Window in Granada" and "A Window in Paris." Small details gathered together from a daily hour or so of watching at a window began to make for me part of the New York picture: a city that stood apart from all others that I had known, as the strangest, the most theatrical, the noisiest, the most written about, and the most unforgettable.

People came and went along the streets, some stayed in one's eyes and thoughts. I remember the elderly scrap dealer, Z. Tickli, that being the name marked on the cart pulled by a slow-paced horse, the only carthorse I saw in use during all my time in New York. Z. Tickli held his own against all the impatient motor vehicles that harassed him. His cart was loaded with old junk, easy enough to collect from almost every city street; the cart made slow but purposeful progress down the crowded city thoroughfares. I am sure that it arrived eventually at wherever Mr. Tickli intended it to arrive.

There were regulars who picked over the dustbin contents on the corner facing our front windows. One of these was a well-dressed lady, who always had on a good-quality fur coat. New York was the only city where I ever saw well-to-do looking people picking over the trash barrels without any sign of embarrassment at what they were doing.

I know that many good things go into the New York trash. In our own case, when I was packing ready for Mexico, there were no poor persons around us to whom I could give our outgrown clothes, or those too shabby to go with us to yet another country. None of our friends had charwomen working for them, "chars" being considered the usual persons to whom one could offer clothes when living in Europe. As for the New York Gypsies whom I had come to know by then, they were all so far better dressed than either my children or myself that I would have felt ashamed to offer them any clothes of ours.

A friend of mine from France, working in New York, was given accommodation in an expensive new apartment house as part of her wages. But during her first years in the city, before she began to earn good money, she clothed herself, and helped many of her friends, with clothing that was thrown down the apartment's rubbish-chute. She inspected the contents twice daily – it was like a treasure hunt for her.

Our own old clothes I made up into parcels and placed on top of the trash containers. I hope that one or other of the trash collectors might have been interested, but I expect that they all earned such good money they could afford to buy new clothes for their families. Many shabby people did pass by on Second Avenue, many looking as if they slept in their clothes, as was probably the case with some of them, with apartments hard to get and the winter weather so cold.

I also saw strange characters, made peculiar by nervous diseases or by drugs or an excess of alcohol. An English artist once published a series of sketches in the *London Graphic* of 1870, showing scenes and people that he had seen while living in New York at that time. *Harper's Weekly* of New York reprimanded him, saying severely that "he either willfully perverted what he saw or else had a singular faculty for seeing what was not observable to ordinary eyes." One picture that gave offense showed, as an example of New York's rag trade, an aged, hag-type woman harnessed with two dogs to a boxlike cart, which was filled with rags.

If I were to describe all the odd types I saw passing below our Second Avenue windows, or that I met with when I was wandering through the city, the same might well be said about my memories of New York life. I never saw so much strangeness elsewhere. I think it must be the extreme tension of city life that causes young women to go out in the streets with disheveled hair, singing silly songs, making antic-like gestures. No one took much notice of them. In most other cities they would have had a crowd following after them, or likely would have been arrested by the police. Then there were the men, often quite well-dressed ones, who walked properly but shouted out crazy things. Not the partly logical cry of an alcoholic-type man whom we saw among a crowd watching a fire on Third Avenue, who cried repeatedly, "Phony fire! Phony fire!" Perhaps he had lit a phony fire once and now accused others? There were many male characters who went along the streets crying out senseless things. The strangest one I heard was on Astor Place, near the subway. A smartly dressed man was waving his arms like a windmill and shouting out: "Upstairs! Downstairs! And my grandmother's corsets!" He repeated this cry endlessly. Again no one laughed or took any notice of him, which seemed so strange to me.

Once, in the early afternoon, I saw standing outside Levine's Comfort Shoes, which faced our building across Second Avenue, a giant and a dwarf. They carried square-shaped parcels. The dwarf might have been able to fit himself with a pair of child's shoes, but the giant, whose head seemed to reach almost to the first-floor window opposite us, would have needed made-to-measure shoes to fit his huge feet. The couple had probably come from a Christmas circus. Fascinated, my children observed them, marveling at the contrast in size.

The odd pair also attracted the attention of a group of teenagers who daily frequented a coffee shop a few doors away from Levine's Shoes. The teenagers were a notable regular street sight from our window. Dressed in bright zipper jackets, often with contrasting sleeves and colored insertions, blue jeans, or bright checks, canvas ankle boots or rubber snow boots, the young people were as restless as houseflies. They came and went out of the coffee shop; they hovered around it. Its door was never still, as the youths and girls came out for "a breather" and then went back again into the steamy interior. They also sat out on the step, or crouched uncomfortably in a row in the small amount of sunlight that filtered down near the shop. For theirs was the sunny side of the street and ours, sadly, was the shady. They chewed gum, almost every one of them, and they shared cigarettes. Quite often they sang glees, making a circle, with heads huddled together (not unlike the way that Spanish Gypsy men sing flamenco sometimes, a group of perhaps six men all urging each other on to excel in that soaring wailing song inherited by the Spanish Gypsies from the Moors of Morocco).

The teenagers sang western songs and others that sounded like songs of the American tramps. Most of them had sweet voices. Sometimes they brought mouth-organs. The gatherings outside the coffee shop were daily, but the singing was not. We never knew when they would sing. We were pleased to hear it. It was sweet and rather sad. I wanted to throw oranges, or bars of candy, down from our windows as thanks, as one does for the Gypsies in Spain. But I felt too shy to do so.

In contrast to the few colorful people who passed by, including the occasional strange beautiful woman or very handsome man, the rest of the crowd were drab as sparrows. Our neighborhood was working-class and principally inhabited by Hungarians, Rumanians, European Jews, some Greeks, and farther uptown, around Yorkville, Irish and Spanish. A typical New York Manhattan mixture was expressed by Morris Abel Beer, who wrote:

> There's Asia on the avenue,
> And Europe in the street,
> And Africa goes plodding by,
> Beneath my window seat.

As it was winter, most of the men wore dull-looking topcoats, with their heads muffled in the popular woolen scarves called *babushkas.* These scarves were on sale in the many Hungarian clothing shops in the neighborhood;

I chose the brightest I could find and posted them off to Gypsy friends in Spain and England. As, during our time on Second Avenue, there was usually snow, or slush, or rain puddles underfoot, most of the people wore snow boots, rubbers, or galoshes, which made a brushing sound passing beneath our windows: one of the sounds of New York to remember.

Would spring ever come? That is a question that one asks every year in every land; and in New York spring comes late. It was an unexpected surprise to see, one Friday morning in mid-February, almond blossoms all along Second Avenue. I shall never forget that sight! The blossoms were on trucks being borne to some unknown destination. The trucks were nameless, odd-looking, gray, and not a mere one or two, but a proud caravan of six passing in procession down Second Avenue, all laden with tossing pink-silver clouds of almond blossoms. Nor was the blossom the usual sparse sprays sold in good-class florist shops in the spring. These were entire boughs, maybe complete trees; a whole grove of flowering almonds cut down to fill those six open trucks. For what purpose would such a quantity of almond blossoms be needed? Those trucks of almond blossoms remain one of the mysteries of New York. What did the truck drivers feel when they looked back and saw clouds of pink and mauve with silver – almond blossoms – massed behind them, and caught the sweet fragrance of that flower, which always holds a faint breath in it of the nuts that it will bear?

The six trucks of almond blossoms passed between sidewalks crowded with people, but all except two elderly women were too busy to stand and stare. The mysterious and lovely cargo passed by almost unnoticed. Yes, spring comes late in cities. A Chinese poet wrote:

> In the capital spring comes late. . . .
> They say it is the time of the peonies,
> So they come together to buy flowers.

We had already come together to buy flowers! As soon as the high Christmas holiday prices were ended, we were searching through the many beautiful flower shops of New York. When it seemed that we would have to be content with wilting twigs of pussy willow, which is the "flower" of the poor in New York, flower prices being sadly high, we found hyacinths in terra-cotta pots at one dollar each. I must, all in all, through two months, have spent twenty dollars on hyacinths. With that money, I could have bought a new jacket, which I needed. But those hyacinths in their peasant-type pots, with the heavy perfume of their flowers filling the apartment, were early springtime to my soul, gathered beauty to my eyes, and, moreover, something to tend, after years without a garden to enjoy. We had a pot of hyacinths at every window of our apartment, and at our favorite window where we street-gazed, we always kept three pots. In ancient lore, Osiris says to Nefertiti of Egypt that humans cannot live very long without the tranquility offered from the perfume of flowers. The main contents of an Indian medicine bag are herbs of sweet smell and of favorite memory, often ones associated with a pleasant place known in childhood.

We took good care of our hyacinths, putting them outdoors into the rays of sunlight that touched the metal stairs of the fire escape outside the window of the back room for a short while each day. At night, for warmth, we used to stand

them in a circle around an electric lamp, and put a fleecy shawl around them, as one might wrap frail human infants. For – as in many New York apartments – all our steam heat was cut off nightly from ten o'clock until six o'clock the following morning: the only hours of true cold in the city, when the temperature often dropped well below zero Farenheit, and when heating was needed the most.

The care that I took of our hyacinths reminded me of lines in a poem by a favorite American writer of mine, Edna St. Vincent Millay:

> I am in love with him/to whom a hyacinth is dearer/
> than I shall ever be dear.

(I have been through that once!)

When new snow fell, we put spoons of it into the hyacinth pots, knowing that it was very good for them. Snow is nature's great fertilizer, rich in phosphates and nitrates; one has only to observe the phosphorescent light of snow to realize this. If the New York snow had come to us through cleaner air, I could have let my children eat amounts of it, mixed with jam, as they have done in other places. The Turkish Gypsies taught me to eat snow with jam when I spent the winter once near Istanbul; and then in America, I learned a snow dish of the early American settlers, who poured hot molasses onto snow and twisted the mixture into thin sticks. A sticky mess which all children will enjoy. Hot maple syrup can also be used, but the snow must be pure. Our Afghan hounds helped themselves to quantities of snow when in New York, in the cleaner places of Central Park. An Afghan will sit down on its haunches like a wolf, and, like a wolf, eat a wide circle of snow all around it.

Springtime brought the window cleaners to New York. A professional thief came to clean ours! He was not a window cleaner at all, but a man who went from apartment to apartment, robbing women. He was a half-caste, with a gray-yellow face, many gold teeth in his mouth, and tight graying curls pushing beneath his trilby hat. He came to me with the plausible story that the owner of the apartment house had recommended him to clean the windows. Therefore, as I had let him into the apartment, I let him carry out the wishes of the proper owner.

He sent me to get soap for him. In other countries window cleaners provide their own materials; however, I supplied a bar of soap as asked. This he smeared on the windows and then declared that it was bad quality and he wanted soap powder instead. Again I went in search. My children were out with our dog. I was feeling such an aura of violence around this man that I kept close to the outside door all the time that I was alone with him, ready to run away outdoors and slam the door behind me if he should threaten me in any way. I was thankful when my children and hound returned. They brought events to a conclusion – for the Afghan hound stepped directly up to the window cleaner and sniffed at his jacket pocket. A shout of rage from the man, declaring that he would not clean windows where there were dirty dogs around and that we must tie up the dog at once. I told my son to do so. The window cleaner then muttered that he must go out for some better soap, and hurried from our apartment, leaving all the front windows well smeared with soap. He also left his cleaning rags on the floor, an old blue shirt torn up into a number of pieces. I at once told my children to look around and see if the window cleaner had taken anything because he appeared to be a bad type of man.

We searched around, but found all things still in place; nothing seemed to be missing. Only the window cleaner himself was missing! He did not return to clean the soap off our windows. When I needed some things from the shops, I went to the well-concealed place where I kept my purse, hanging behind a screen, mixed up with dog leads, luggage straps, and so forth. My purse was still there. But when I went into the first shop and made ready to pay for my purchases, I found it had been emptied of all the money, nearly fifty dollars. The window cleaner, in the clairvoyant way of the professional thief, had known within the few minutes allotted to him while I searched for the soap where to find my purse! And again like the professional thief, he had taken only the money, and left the purse.

The loss of fifty dollars was a blow to me at that time, otherwise the incident would have been funny. I have since learned the New York way of keeping one's door on a chain so that when the doorbell is rung one can peer out, with the chain barring entry to all callers, and only admit people who are trusted. Door-to-door salesmen must have a hard time with those chained doors of the housewives! I also gained for myself a lecture from the New York police, for daring to let an unknown man into my apartment while I was there alone, and therefore helping to make profitable the work of the criminal class operating in New York.

When I told the police that, as a writer with necessarily observant eyes, I could give them a detailed description of the thief, they said they did not need that, they already knew him down to the smallest detail: He had been a wanted man for a long time. I then told them that I had, untouched, still in my possession, the man's cleaning cloths. My education in crime progressed, for I was told that cloth does not hold fingerprints well and is useless for clues.

In contrast to the locking and chaining of doors in New York City, friends of mine in country houses a short drive from New York never lock their doors. Some friends in nearby Connecticut lost their house keys years ago and never replaced them. [Editor's note: My house in the Catskills, one hundred miles north of Manhattan, has no locks. When I lived in the city, I had three locks on every door and two on each window.]

My children found a new pastime resulting from the visit of the thief. Whenever we went into a New York post office, they would seek out the sheaf of papers pinned up there, giving "Wanted" photos and descriptions. They were searching for the ugly face of the window cleaner. I wish we had let our Afghan hound have her way with him – we might not have lost our fifty dollars.

The next excitement was our witnessing of a big fire in the city. That is, a fire big enough to be reported on the radio and to appear on New York television and in the newspapers. The first warning to us of the incident was a remarkable blackening of the sky, so that I thought we were going to witness a cyclone, although it was the wrong time of the year, and unlike Mexico, New York was really not the right geographical place for one. Then at the same time, we smelled smoke and heard the clamor of many racing fire engines.

Even if the eccentric behavior of people abroad in the streets of New York, the glee-singers on the sidewalks, and trucks of almond blossoms fail to attract interest, a big fire is like a magnet. Large crowds were soon hastening toward Third Avenue, where the fire was said to be. It was on East 81st Street, therefore not far from us on East 78th Street. The news was soon passed around that people had been trapped in the burning building and rescued by a news photographer named Lockhart.

The fire had broken out on the second floor of a furniture store and quickly burned upwards to the other floors, finally to burst through the roof. It was well fed on foam-rubber mattresses and similar inflammable materials. Hence the blackness and great volume of the smoke that had darkened the sky. We could see firemen using hatchets to break the windows of neighboring houses and lead people away from smoke suffocation. A helicopter hovered overhead; some people said it was pouring water, others that it was taking photos, or giving advice to the firemen as to the spread of the fire. It was interesting to observe the remarkable efficiency of New York's famed fire service. They were striving to prevent the fire from spreading to a vast moving and storage firm that adjoined the furniture store.

Everyone was tense as they watched – police and spectators, anxious and caring – except for that one strange man who cried out monotonously, "Phony fire! Phony fire!" until the police sent him away for being a public nuisance.

We saw the tall flames vanquished under the storm of hissing water directed upon them, and everyone rejoiced that the big depository had not been touched at all by the dangerous fire. It had been a splendid sight, from the fire flames themselves to the fire engines and their crews. No one had been hurt, and real-life theater had been provided on a Manhattan street. When we passed by that way again a short time later, workmen were already rebuilding the burned-out store. Property in Manhattan was too valuable to be left empty. Where only a few hundred years back had been but a half dozen huts built by the first Dutch settlers, there now stood a concrete kingdom so valuable that its base almost has the value of solid gold.

As we returned from the scene of the Third Avenue fire, in the dusk, I marveled, as I have marveled many times before, on the quality of the evening light over this city. How the shape and density of all objects is transformed, and perspective and measurable distances both are mysteriously modified.

How typical of New York City that we ourselves had an artificial light to guide us home, no North Star as we often followed in other country places, but a flashing sign above the store that adjoined the rear of the apartment house in which we lived. The sign that flashed out to guide us home was "Wines, Liquors." That was our sign for the time being.

Mme. Heredia, instructor in sorcery; Marseilles Gypsy quarter

Chapter Three

The Gypsies Make Their Living

The first Gypsy family I came to know in New York was the Markovitch family of fortune tellers, on Second Avenue. Our doorkeeper friend outside the club Roma di Notte, on Second Avenue, stopped us one evening to tell us that "some of your people have arrived on the avenue and have opened a fortune-telling place there."

The doorkeeper was a Hungarian, and we often talked together about Gypsies in his own country. He was a great admirer of our Afghan hound Cingane, which means "Gypsy" in Turkish. Her kennel and registered name was "Turkuman Nissam's Halfa Grass." Man and hound always greeted each other with affection when we passed by the club.

The *ofisa* of the Markovitches was toward Yorkville, and I expected would be patronized largely by the Spanish and Puerto Ricans whose neighborhood adjoined there. Written in white paint on the window were the words that one finds on most of the American Gypsy fortune-telling stores: "Se Habla Español" (Spanish spoken). To describe the *ofisa* of the Markovitches is to describe all other such places, for they are of identical pattern and are quite plentiful along Lexington Avenue, Third, Sixth, and Eighth Avenues, as well as being numerous in Harlem and Brooklyn.

These *ofisas* are also often called "Gypsy tearooms," and a cup of tea is usually sold to clients as part of the fortune-telling rite, although tea-leaves readings are scorned by the true deep Gypsy fortune tellers and are considered something for the uninitiated amateur.

The cup of tea is a mere formality to justify money being charged in case there comes trouble with the police. There are several cafes in New York called "The Gypsy Tearoom," named after the Gypsy *ofisa*.

The shop window of the Markovitch place had the typical Gypsy part-magic, part-religious motif. There were, set out in the window, books on dreams, also three magic books with Spanish titles: a book of White Magic, a book of Black Magic, and a book of Green Magic. Later, when I examined and read through the books, I saw that they had been printed in Mexico, Mexico City to be exact. I had never before met with green magic!

The green magic was mostly concerned with the powers of herbs and with accounts of great magicians. Included was Paracelsus, the great medieval doctor, who wandered the world in the company of Gypsies and wrote many famed books on magic. Only I was surprised to see also the name of Maimonides, the honored Jewish rabbi and doctor, tutored by the Moors of Spain, who became chief physician to the Saracen conqueror and ruler, Saladin, the green-turbaned, wonderful Arab.

Also, I was interested to find in the green magic book an ancient herbal recipe that I have often used and found very effective, employing one of my favorite herbs, rosemary, called "Queen of Hungary's Water." It soothes headaches, calms shattered nerves, and brings sleep. I often felt in need of some Queen of Hungary's Water while living in New York! But the mountain slopes that I knew, where wild rosemary could be gathered, were far away from me – in southern Spain, Galilee, and Mexico – and the little rosemary offered to me in herbalist shops in America was so yellowed and highly priced that I refused to purchase any. If I had had time to search in the botanical shops of Spanish Harlem, I could likely have found better. Here's the recipe:

Queen of Hungary's Water

2 pounds of flowering shoots of fresh rosemary
3 pints of alcohol

Place together in a closed vessel in a warm place (in the sunlight or by a hot stove) for 50 hours, adding to these hours day by day until the fifty are completed. Then strain and bottle. To prevent evaporation, some almond oil can be added as a layer on top of the liquid. [Apply to the face with the fingertips.]

Another good recipe, well known to Gypsies, is the Vinegar of Four Thieves, *Vinaigre de Quatre Voleurs.* It is used as a lotion to steal away all muscular pain and cramps; and a few drops on a piece of cloth or bread will revive fainting persons, give courage to the faint-hearted, and cure depression.

Vinegar of Four Thieves

2 ounces each of fresh or dried tops of
rosemary (*Rosmarinus off.*)
wormwood (*Artemisia absinthimum*)
dill (*Anethum graveolens*)
sage (*Salvia off.*)
mint (*Mentha species*)
rue (*Ruta graveolens*)
lavender (*Lavendula species*)

Cover with strong natural vinegar (not malt vinegar), about one gallon (8 pounds). Macerate the herbs in the vinegar for a fortnight, then strain, pressing well. Combine two ounces of acetic acid and add ½ ounce of camphor dissolved in some water. Add to vinegar; shake very well together. *For external use only.*

There were religious figures in the *ofisa* window: Virgin with child, and what appeared to be Saint Joseph. There were texts on the wall, such things as "God Bless This House," "God is Love," and others of that kind. Draped curtains partitioned the fortune-telling side of the store from the rear, where the family lived, cooked, dined, and slept. The *ofisa* part was further divided up into cupboard-size places, like confession cubicles in a church. In these places clients had their hands read and had some magic and religion, both mixed like the decorations of the *ofisa*, practiced upon them. "If you ill, I pray for you. If you have friend ill, I pray for he. If you without love, I bring you love."

I wonder why the Bible Society of New York never printed the Bible in Romany, international language of the Gypsies? They have translated the Bible into eighty-two languages, but not Romany. Perhaps they decided that, as so few Gypsies can read, a Romany Bible would be a waste of time and money. Language experts consider Romany, Gypsy "talking," to be the oldest extant language surviving in the world today. It is called a "talking language" because it is seldom written. However, that fine character George Borrow, traveler, writer, and *Romany Rye* (a non-Gypsy who befriends the Gypsies), did translate quite large portions of the Bible into Gypsy language. His own books of travel, *The Bible in Spain* and *Wild Wales*, should be read as companions to his classics *Romany Rye* and *Lavengro.*

There is often candlelight in the *ofisas* during hand-reading, and incense may be used. But in the back room there is probably television, and the set is kept in action most of the day, whether people are watching it or not. Most of my conversations with Caterina Markovitch were conducted to a background of television: boxing matches, horse races, floor shows, and American advertising. I found the same situation in many of the other *ofisas.*

When I first met Caterina she was sitting by her window, sewing curtains. When I spoke some Romany to her she greeted me with excitement, abandoned her sewing, and took me into the rear of her store, to drink coffee with her family. She had seven children: the eldest ones were not with her in New York; the middle ones helped with the hand-readings. The youngest, little Mimi, lay on a bed of cushions in a corner of the room, sick with fever. The steam heating and general airlessness of the place were blamed for this. The family had recently come by road from Los Angeles.

The daughters – Linda and Alicia – who were fortune tellers, were very handsome young women. They always wore Gypsy clothes: headscarves, long-skirted dresses, and much jewelry. Alicia had something of the witch in her, and was apt to will away from people more dollars than they had intended to pay for having their hands read by her. It was interesting for me that my daughter, Luz Alicia, shared her name. It is said of Gypsies of her kind, that when they ask for money, it is with such consummate skill and such a power of will behind their desire, that the victim is often fascinated into willing compliance.

One way of getting the client to part with money is for the fortune teller to ask for a large note to be placed in her hand during the reading, "to bring the powers of good luck and clear seeing." The usual fee of two dollars is also charged before the reading commences. At the conclusion of the reading, the larger money note is not returned. This is especially used on young men. If a man causes "trouble," the woman fortune teller declares that he offered her the money with amorous advances, and she took it from him.

Of all the numerous New York friends whom I introduced to Gypsy fortune tellers, only one had such a trick played upon him. It cost him ten dollars, which he lost to Alicia!

I promised Caterina to bring my collection of Gypsy photographs to show her. I had taken them with Gypsies of many lands, and what was of interest to the Gypsies was that my children appeared in many of them, sitting on horses with wild-looking Gypsies of the Spanish mountains, or at the horse and mule fairs with a crowd of naked Yugoslav Gypsy children, or outside Gypsy vans in France, or sitting with roadside Gypsies in England, and so on, showing that the Gypsy photos were of my own taking and not merely obtained from others. Those photos were really my "visiting cards" to leave with new Gypsy friends.

An interesting fact is that in all the years that I have passed them around from Gypsy hands to Gypsy hands, much as they have wanted them and have often asked me for one or another of them, not one photo has been taken

Luz and Rafik with two Gypsies.

from my collection. The negatives were long ago stored away in some distant place, I know not where, and I could not replace the photos if any were taken. It was strange afterwards to look through my collection and see the ones that most interested the New York Gypsies – they certainly recognized their own kind! Those that they had fingermarked most, and crumpled the corners of most, showed Hungarian and Rumanian Gypsies at the Gypsy fiesta of Les Saintes Maries, in French Provence; they were also attracted by my photos of the French Camargue "Apache" Gypsies of Alsace-Lorraine, again much like themselves in physical type and way of life.

I found that Caterina could *dukker* (read hands) with skill: She read my hand in exchange for my reading hers! On one thing she was very definite, that my Galilee book – at the time being read by American publishers – would be accepted for publication. [Now available in a new edition from Ash Tree Publishing.] As I was well aware of the overcrowding in the world of American writers, I felt very uncertain of my own chances. But Caterina was clear: "No doubt at all; it is promised!" Before I left New York – and I was leaving without waiting for the results of my literary agent's negotiations – my Gypsy friend was proved right.

The husbands of the Markovitch girls often came into the store when their tasks of relining metal boilers were done for the day. They liked to discuss with me Gypsy life in other lands. They are proud of their Gypsy race and feel that their own people are superior to most others because they are among the freest of all, and freedom is the highest prize that any man could possess. Nonetheless, nowadays some of the town Gypsies of America, especially in Chicago, who have large families to earn for, are accepting employment in factories.

A Mr. Sam Epstein told me his experience of unknowingly employing five Gypsy brothers in his factory for manufacturing aircraft parts. Short of hands, he took in five men from the local labor exchange (Americans would probably call it something else). He imagined from their dark and handsome faces that they were Greeks, as, in addition to their very odd-sounding English, they spoke among themselves in a language unknown to him.

Soon they brought disorder to his factory, and it was remarkable that they could do so, because his factory was large and well-organized. Because of the nature of the merchandise, absolute order was essential at all times in all departments. Small airplane parts began to appear in the wrong places; there was unusual singing and noise in the factory; doors were left open and windows everywhere were opened, thus causing duststorms, blowing away of papers, and so forth. The five brothers came to work at any time they chose, left at any time, and could never be found in their proper places in the factory. When reprimanded on these counts, the stories that all of them told in their own defense were "so harrowing, so dramatic," declared Mr. Epstein, "that they crept up one's arteries into one's very heart, and dollars were handed out to comfort the unfortunate men in their sorrows!"

But despite those sad stories, after a week of near havoc in the factory, the five new workers were dismissed. They took with them large supplies of good clothing, canned foods, and other useful goods, which their fellow workers at the factory, likewise moved by their touching stories, had readily provided!

Later, when the same men had created similar disorder in a friend's factory, Mr. Epstein found out they were Czechoslovakian Gypsies. He said that their strange actions in his factory had seemed to him like the policy of the Russians in politics: achieve power by creating confusion. "Their behavior was confusing, unreasonable, and completely unpredictable, therefore it caused apprehension and finally fear in the persons in contact with them."

I personally feel that the five Gypsies were merely being rebellious at having to suffer factory employment to provide for their families. The true Gypsy soul is lost in a factory.

D. H. Lawrence possessed the soul of a Gypsy and he understood the Romanies very well. He wrote about the age-old and peculiar battle that the Gypsies wage against established society. He says that the Gypsies possess an air of silent and forever unyielding outsideness. In his brilliant novel, *The Virgin and the Gypsy*, he writes of "the pride of the pariah, the half-sneering challenge of the outcast who sneered at law-abiding men and went his own way."

In New York I met a Gypsy taxi driver. My children and I were taking quite a long ride from upper Second Avenue to the outskirts of Greenwich Village. I noted that the taxi driver was very dark, wore his hair in the long sideburns typical of many Gypsy men, and that, despite the winter day being a very cold one, he had the neck of his shirt wide open. A Gypsy wearing a tight necktie is a rarity. They seek freedom in clothing. The women do not wear brassieres or corsets. The men wear open-necked shirts, or sometimes that traditional adornment of the Gypsy male, the *dicklow* (a short neck scarf loosely tied). A paisley design in bright colors is the most favored for *dicklows.*

Paisley belongs to the Gypsies: it is their chosen pattern, that and the lunaris luna moon, an all-over pattern of tiny circles, much used by the Gypsy women dancers of Granada.

I conveyed my notion that he might be a Gypsy to the taxi driver in an undirect way by asking, "Do you ever get Gypsy fares?"

He laughed, and, pointing at my two children and me, he threw back at me, "I've got three now!"

That made it easier to talk Gypsy with him. "You look like a Gypsy yourself," I then ventured. With persecuted races, especially Jews and Gypsies, it is often unwelcome for one's race to be revealed by a stranger. Only in Israel and New York, where there is such a high percentage of Jews, and they have absolute freedom from racial discrimination, have I met people who say at once: "I am Jewish."

"And right you are, too!" the taxi driver said. I had met my first Gypsy taxi driver, although I believe there are many of them in Russia and Hungary. In Granada, Spain, I came to know several Gypsy policemen. They would always, in friendship, hold up the busy traffic for me and my Afghan hound to cross the roads. The same happened in Turkey.

On his taxi license his name was Elkan, although, he told me, his original Serbian family name had been Elkanovitch. Most of the Romanian, Slovakian, and Serbian Gypsies whom I came to know in New York had the "vitch" ending to their names, although Illynavitch had become Williams, and Nikkolovitch is now Nichols!

We talked about Gypsies together. Boris Elkan had been a professional entertainer to the troops during World War II. He had played the guitar and sung popular songs. He told me about a handsome young boy who had persistently asked him to let him join him as an entertainer; at last he gave the boy a hearing and found that he could sing and dance with brilliance, and play the violin as well as any concert-hall violinist that Elkan had ever heard. Therefore he took the boy along with him on his war travels. Once they were back in America together, on leave, and the boy invited Elkan home to meet his people in far South Carolina. Elkan found himself in a Hungarian Gypsy encampment where a large feast was prepared to welcome the two soldiers back home. He would never forget that feast! The family was delighted to find that their son had teamed up with a fellow Gypsy and had not had to kill any person (as yet), and they excelled themselves in that celebration. An enormous fire was lit, and a dozen young pigs were put to roast on a long iron rod over the fire. Wine was so plentiful that it was poured into buckets, and loaves of bread were piled up in a pyramid as big as a Gypsy *tan* (tent). And there was the most superb Gypsy dancing and fiddle music.

Long after we had reached the dress shop of our friends, Florence and Rosemary Molinari in the village, we sat talking in Elkan's taxi. He switched off the meter, and we just sat and talked. He told me how pleased he was when he had country visits to undertake for fares. Then as soon as he was rid of the fares, he would take off his boots and walk about barefoot on the grass and get a nice switch of grass to chew on, and look around for some supplies of good country foods such as wild greens and berries and farm produce.

Later, in New York, we heard about preparations for another kind of Gypsy feast, a funeral feast. Mary Illynavitch Williams, of Lexington Avenue, described it to me.

We would not be in New York at the time of the wake, as I was taking over the care of a herd of goats in Baja California, Mexico, and had to be there to get them into a good state of health before they gave birth to their kids in April and May. Therefore we had to be content with a mere description of that New York Gypsy event.

The Gypsy's words widened the eyes of my listening children. From the time of the death, there was held a wake on every six: first the sixth day, then the sixth month, and then the big funeral feast on the twelfth month, which is the double six. A young man from a wealthy Boston Gypsy family had died, and now the important anniversary of his death was to be celebrated. The wake was to be held in New York because most of the dead man's family were there, and also many more Gypsies to make the feast a memorable one. All the love for the dead was put into such feasts. A large hall had been hired already, and every New York Gypsy was welcome to attend. We had already been invited.

The dead man's family were known to be bringing with them three whole dressed pigs, about a dozen live geese, several hundred chickens, and many hares. I sorrowed for all those animals being shipped alive, a journey of terror, and then at the end, a violent death: the knife. Much wine, bread, and pastry would be purchased in New York. Then, above all, the Gypsies were bringing with them a new suit of clothes costing five hundred dollars. That price amazed my children, as they knew the small prices we could afford for clothes when travel costs took away so much of my money every year. The magnificent new suit would be a gift from the dead man to the person of his own family blood who best fitted into the suit.

We came to know Mary Illynavitch by chance during our first winter in New York, and she became my favorite of all the Gypsy families we knew. We were attracted to a curio shop on Lexington Avenue, owned by a Mr. Yervant, who I learned was an Armenian, born in Turkey. He had strange things in his shop, including many tiny model animals, of which I bought several. On our first approach to his shop door, Mr. Yervant waved his hand at us, indicating that we should go up the stairs adjoining his place. We did as directed and on the first floor found ourselves outside a Gypsy fortune-teller's apartment, with "Madame Valiant" written on the door. Within was Mary Illynavitch, who gave us an affectionate welcome and invited us to return that evening to meet her family, who would all be at home by then. That I agreed to do.

We then went into the Yervant shop to look at the curios, which were very good. Mr. Yervant told us that he had taken us to be more Gypsy visitors for the Illynavitch family, who had only moved into the first-floor apartment recently and had had a procession of Gypsy visitors to and fro to them ever since. He said that in the Illynavitch family there was an old Gypsy woman who was a great character, that she looked like a walking curio shop as she carried so much jewelry upon her person, including much fine coral; that she was very "gallant," and every weekend, when the avenue was busy, she would be out on the sidewalk asking passing men for a light for her cigarette, and then handing them one of Madame Valiant's advertising bills, announcing the Gypsy fortune-telling *ofisa*; that he had seen her bring in many men that way. Mr. Yervant liked the Gypsies well enough, and he told me that he had a personal association with the race. For while his mother, in a Turkish village, had been in labor for his birth, the Gypsies had been dancing outside the window all the time, cheering and encouraging her. And even today, any kind of wild behavior he might indulge in was blamed on the spell of the Turkish Gypsies who had danced at his birth.

On our return to Lexington Avenue, the old Gypsy, an aunt, was there, and she fascinated my children and me. She had been summoned by telephone especially to meet us. Most of the New York fortune-telling Gypsies have telephones, all except those that I came to know in the Bowery. It is strange to hear the Gypsies speaking their own Romany language over the telephone, just as strange as it was to find telephone and electric lighting in most of the mountain caves of the Gypsy dancers of Granada, Spain. Small Gypsy children would also talk in Romany to their family on the telephone, both in New York and Granada, where Gypsies have commercialized their talents, the fortune-telling in the American city and the dancing in the Spanish.

The aunt had the strange and splendid name of Barrabas, which sounded like a masculine name to me. She was garbed in full and traditional Gypsy dress, and she jingled with jewelry, as Mr. Yervant had described. Her jewels were not the coral or turquoise favored by the Gypsies, and of which things, especially coral, the Romanies possess the world's finest collection, as they have been collecting it in all lands through the ages. Barrabas's jewelry was old silver, wonderfully wrought and set with hand-cut natural stones, which she told me had come to her from the American Indians, with whom she had been very friendly. She sold their home-made medicines from door to door in many parts of America, buying cheaply from the native people and selling at good profit to white families, long before the coming of the village drugstore. She had done fortune-telling along with the medicine trading, too. And found the American Indians deeply interested, only as they – like the Gypsies – possess the powers of seeing and prophecy, they would often take over their own readings and tell the fortune teller what she should be seeing!

Barrabas was of true Gypsy type, of willowy slenderness, tall and weather-worn like the figurehead of an old ship; with dark, hard flesh, finely lined like the graining of old wood, her gold teeth many, flashing in the electric light of the apartment, adding to her figurehead look. Many of the people of the Gypsy tribes found in New York – the Serbians, the Kalderash (Russian and Serbian coppersmiths), the Romanian, Hungarian, and Polish – possess many gold teeth. That gold in their mouths cost many of them their lives in Nazi-occupied countries where the Gypsies had been numerous.

The niece, Mary, was very unlike her aunt, being fat and white; only her deep-set eyes, dark and glittering as chips of onyx, indicated her Gypsy race. When I commented on the great difference between the two Gypsies, Barrabas said truly: "She is of the new Romany life, of the *kairs* an' the *kens* (houses and towns), while I am of the old, of the *tans* (tents). Wait till you see her daughter, an' my favorite niece, our Anna, then tell me what you think!"

From the old one's words I expected that the Gypsy girl, Anna, would be one of the made-up type of New York teenagers, only this proved not to be so at all. When Anna joined the company of ten Gypsies now gathered in the apartment, a real Romany beauty entered. It was true that she was white-skinned like her mother, and there was no weathering on her face, but she was true Gypsy. How beautiful! She was wearing a homemade parma violet satin dress, earrings of gold coins on chains were shining among locks of carbon-black hair, pearls glowed round her full white neck. She was seventeen. Her hair shone as brilliantly as the plumage of the big crows, and when I asked her about this she told me that it was dressed not with the traditional hedgehog grease of the Gypsies but with ordinary

Moka, Lola, El Chaquete, La Mariposa dance; Granada olive grove

stove paraffin. That was what set her hair and gave it the shine. Strange information!

Anna reminded me of the Gypsy girl Preciosa, in Cervantes's *La Gitanilla*: "When Preciosa beats her tambourine and the sweet music wounds the empty air, it is pearls that drop from her hands, flowers that she sends from her mouth."

In this same book about the Spanish Gypsies, Cervantes has Preciosa say to a non-Gypsy: "Our mind is different from yours: our understanding makes us older than our years. We sail over strange waters and plot our course by a Pole-star that is unknown to you. And you will never find a foolish Gypsy man or a simple Gypsy woman. In truth there is no Gypsy girl twelve years old who does not know more than a Spanish lady of twenty-five."

Mary told me that there was a crazy artist living in the building several floors up, and he kept bringing her family unwelcome gifts for the opportunity of gazing at Anna. He was an ugly man and not a good artist, and she was told by others in the building that no one bought the pictures he painted. Mary did not like to go out and leave her daughter alone in the apartment in case the artist broke in. Her daughter had already traveled most of America and was able to take care of herself in the usual way, but one could never be sure of the actions of a mad man!

I felt sorry for the artist, so mad, so much in love with the beautiful young Gypsy, and no one buying his pictures.

It was late evening when we arrived at the Illynavitch *ofisa*, but the meal was still cooking and I felt sure that they had kept it so late for us to share it with them. I had specially delayed our visit until I felt they would have finished their evening meal.

The cooking arrangements were as near to a Gypsy campfire as could be managed in a New York apartment. The place was well furnished and expensive-looking, with wall-to-wall carpeting, good modern furniture, and the usual television set. There were the typical curtain drapings behind which the family slept, possibly on the floor on the usual mattress rolls; I could not see into the sleeping part of the place.

For the cooking, there was a small metal sheet on the floor on one side of the room, and on this was placed a square, electric, box-type heating ring, which was now holding a large iron pot from which meaty fumes came.

Mary instructed her daughter Anna and the two younger girls to prepare the table for supper. This merely consisted of spreading sheets of newspaper in a square around the cooking stove, and onto this were put a soup plate for each diner, which included my family of three, and a wooden spoon by each plate. Mary told me that they were Gypsy spoons, which her brother had made. Three long loaves of dark rye bread, a pot of salt, and a pot of olive oil were next placed on the table, and the Gypsies then told us to be seated. So we all sat on the floor, in front of a portion of the newspaper, and Mary Illynavitch began to ladle out the contents of the big black pot. This seemed to be a typical Gypsy stew. Lumps of meat were mixed up with all types of vegetables: carrots, onions, turnips, and parsnips predominating, from what I could see.

I had to tell Mary that my children and I are vegetarians and never eat meat, and that we would be very satisfied with the bread and oil. There was no argument from her, no trying to persuade me to change our dietary law for that one time, or to tell me that it was cruel to deprive my children of meat, as I am often told when invited to eat in other people's houses (and despite my children's noticeably strong bodies). She merely said, "Then you will eat cheese," and told Anna to put on her coat and go to a shop. I protested that it was not necessary to go to such trouble, that we had eaten before coming to the avenue. But Mary insisted, and Anna put on her fine fur coat, which was not at all in keeping with the rest of her Gypsy dress but suited her very well. Soon she returned with a whole cheese, from which Mary Williams cut us pieces big enough to feed us for one week, not for one meal! There were two Gypsy lads in the party, the rest were women and girls.

We talked about notable Gypsies in New York, about the various Dukes and Kings of the various Gypsy tribes, and about such characters as Django Reinhart, the wonderful jazz musician who had sadly died young, and Romany Marie, formerly a friend of nearly every writer and painter in Greenwich Village, who had forsaken a forest in Moldavia for a store on Delancey Street. Her father had been a tavern-keeper in the old country, and she herself had been in demand as an artist's model on coming to America. Later she managed a successful tavern in Greenwich Village, where the non-Gypsy Bohemians liked to gather. She never forsook her own Gypsy people and was always ready to help Gypsies. She would often let the Gypsy wanderlust possess her, when she would leave the Village and travel the roads again in search of green fields and clean streams, such as the soul of the true Gypsy needs.

Our first Gypsy meal in New York was notable for the absence of American canned, cartoned, or packaged foods such as most modern families use. We finished off our meal with sweet bronzed apples, the very color of the flesh of the many Gypsies present. The apples were passed around in a typical Gypsy wicker basket, and the basket in turn was filled from a tall wooden tub packed with apples in sawdust. Mary said that they had brought them with them from the country. She also said that her family still went out into the New York countryside whenever it was green, and brought back quantities of nettle, dandelion, mustard greens, and wild salad things. They also gathered, every autumn, quantities of chestnuts and mushrooms, which they ate and dried.

I remarked to Mary Illynavitch on the typical Gypsy preference for dark bread, and she said that the good dark bread accounted for the strong teeth of the Gypsies, and for their good eyes, and that eyeglasses were still almost unknown among her people.

I then told the Gypsy company an experience that I had had in England, concerning dark bread and Hungarian Gypsies. At the time of the quite recent Russian occupation of many parts of Hungary, three Gypsy families who had previously survived the Nazis joined the Hungarian refugees seeking homes in England. These Gypsies were sent to a refugee camp in the English Midlands, at Evesham. There they were soon in trouble with the camp officials, who reported that they could do nothing with the Gypsies, who would not speak to anyone and passed their days in sulky and rebellious behavior. My book on my life with foreign Gypsies, *As Gypsies Wander*, was recommended by someone associated with the Hungarian refugees, and through the Gypsy Lore Society of England, they contacted me and offered to pay all my expenses for a visit to the camp. I decided to go there and to take my two children with me on yet one more Gypsy visit. I would rely on some Gypsy Romany and French to speak with the Hungarian Gypsies, who, I was informed, knew no English at all.

So I went to the camp in its setting of blossoming plum orchards, Evesham being one of the chief fruit areas of England. The sulky faces of the Hungarian Gypsies were soon laughing ones. The help that they needed had been simple to arrange. They were sulking and rebelling against the tight footwear with which they had been supplied and had been unable to change, and they were hungry for good, nourishing brown, not white, bread. A change of footwear and some good bread were soon provided, together with a promise from the camp authorities that the Gypsies would continue to have the brown bread that they were starving for.

The Gypsies and I arranged a small celebration for the breaking of the first loaves of brown bread provided for them at the camp. I sent one of the Gypsy lads to the nearest shop for butter and some of the famed local plum jam, and I sent another in search of beer and ginger ale. And, as the time was spring, I went out into the fields with the Gypsies and we collected quantities of edible wild plants, for a real Gypsy salad. Dandelion (*Taraxacum off.*), clover (*Trifolium pratense*), plantain (*Plantago species*) and mustard greens were found in abundance, and there were also primrose (*Primula*) leaves and flowers, sorrel (*Rumex acetosella*), chickweed (*Stellaria media*), and hedge-garlic (*Alliaria officinalis*). The last, a new one to them, is not a true garlic plant at all, but is of the mustard family. It is also called "sauce-alone" because it has so many flavors: garlic, mustard, salt, and pepper. We also collected true "Salt and Pepper," which is the young shoots of hawthorn bushes, which possess a salty-peppery taste. The Gypsies introduced me to the young leaves of willow and elm as being good-tasting and edible; one learns new things as one travels and meets strangers.

We spread our feast beneath the blossoming plum trees. The Hungarian Gypsies then offered me an unexpected reward for the small help that I had given them. They brought out their violins and played that special, tearful, love-full music of the Hungarian Gypsies. Their violins, all four, were travel-battered, but in the hands of the true musicians that they were, the music came in the air sweet and clear and sad, and as far-carrying as the voices of a crowd of golden plovers.

Later, I asked the Gypsies to repeat their violin music for the Woman's Voluntary Society lady, and they did so. I then arranged with the Birmingham Broadcast station for the camp Gypsies to play their violins for a series of broadcasts. Their beautiful, soulful music was much admired, and they were well paid; so a happy ending.

All the Gypsies in the Illynavitch apartment then began to amuse us with their own type of Serbian Gypsy entertainment. Songs in Romany and Hrvatski, a Serbo-Croatian language, and their special dances, but also, intermingled, the luring, sensual stepping of their own people. On a later evening I was to take some American friends, Bo and Gareen Shay, Florine Molinari, and Macdonald White (of the Associated Press) to meet some Gypsy friends on Houston Street, in the Bowery. They were also delighted and fascinated by these same dances and songs of other Serbian Gypsies, the Niccolovi (Nichols) family at Madame Star's.

When it was turned midnight we heard a heavy knocking on the Illnavitch apartment door, and all the Gypsies declared that it must be the mad artist!

They told me that they have a special sound for the door, and when they hear that they do not delay to open, for they know it is not an interfering policeman (*gendarmi*), or some other person (from true client to "snooper"). They showed me their special knock. It came like the quick drumming of a woodpecker on a tree.

Soon they opened the door to admit the persistent knocker. And then they all laughed and exclaimed, "Peleg! Welcome, Peleg!" Another Gypsy had arrived, and he had rapped in the non-Gypsy way to tease them. The newcomer was a handsome young man wearing expensive-looking rather flashy clothes, his lilac-colored nylon socks being very conspicuous. I expect that he was one of Anna's suitors, for their eyes met across the room.

We had to leave soon after Peleg's arrival, for it was very late. I knew that on the bus back home I would meet the disapproval of other women passengers because I was keeping my children out so long after the usual bedtime hours. Only, as I said to my children, "Let the people frown! Does it matter if the hours have turned late when we've enjoyed such a very good time with the Gypsies again?"

Gypsy heart, Gypsy music, Gypsy dancing!

Chapter Four

Out of the Everywhere

Gypsies of New York! Gypsies of the World! What can one say about them that has not been said before, and further, how can one be too emphatic about the many facets of Gypsy lore that are "known" and yet so elusive?

Gypsy origin remains a mystery. Despite the skill of modern historical and scientific research into the origins of the peoples of the world, the Gypsies still baffle the anthropologist. Indeed, the Gypsies themselves do not seem to know their own beginnings; that is why one of the first things that Gypsy friends ask me, when they know I have traveled and met their people in many different lands, is: "From where do you think we came? From where? From where?"

It is a mystery! And perhaps the Gypsies, commercial dealers in magic through the ages, like to foster this great mystery. One wonders what reason suddenly brought great bands of Gypsies out from "nowhere" to travel the world. Or maybe not from nowhere, but from their mysterious, legendary land said to be beyond where the sun sets, the opposite direction to the birthplace of the American Indians, who say they come from near where the sun rises.

Early accounts of the Gypsies, when they appeared outside Asia, say they were at first sympathetically received in all the new lands that they entered. Their true or feigned state of penitence gained sympathy: They came as pilgrims traveling to far lands to be released from some religious penalty believed to be associated with the Holy Family. They attracted also admiration and astonishment with their lofty titles of kings, princes, and dukes, and on account of the fine animals – horses, greyhounds, goats, and tamed wild creatures – that they brought with them. But the Gypsies, in common with many nomad races, soon squandered the riches which they had. Then, in a state of poverty, they acquired the contempt of their host populations, especially when the Gypsies began to prey upon their hosts like gaudy parasitic flowers that suck the sap from other plants for sustenance and do not care to strive to make food for themselves.

Almost all the host countries began to turn on them, deriding and penalizing the strangers. The Gypsies were especially punished on account of the occult arts that they practiced, including what was considered "black" magic – by virtue of which they took large sums of money from the populations of both town and countryside.

The Gypsies suffered great hardships and persecution during the Middle Ages, a period of history characterized by injustice and brutality to minorities. They had edict upon edict passed against them: "A race of black magicians and heathens all!" In England there is still sung, along the Border Countries, the ancient "Lament of the Gypsy Faas." This old song was created from a true incident.

In 1624, Helen Faa – direct descendent of Johnny Faa of Scotland, who was recognized by King James I of England, and likewise by the Crown, as being Lord and Count of all the Egyptians (Gypsies) of England – was condemned, together with fifteen more of the seed royal, to public death by drowning in the sea: "For reason of them being Gypsies and having been told – they and all other Egyptians (Gypsies) to leave the shores of England forever, and having failed to obey this order."

They were all bound with chains to prevent their swimming and put in an open boat on a stormy day and pushed out to sea, so that their death by drowning at sea be fulfilled, and it was. Ruthless! As recently as the seventeenth century, Gypsies were punished in some places for slight offenses by being branded on face or back with red-hot irons.

The Gypsies were subjected to more cruel persecution in our present time when the Nazis condemned the whole Gypsy race in all the countries that the Germans occupied (which included Hungary, where the Gypsies were especially numerous). They exterminated them by shooting, gassing, or the slower death of being used for unnatural medical experiments, their renowned good health being a reason for that vile use.

Why is it then, despite worldwide, age-old persecution in most of the lands through which the Gypsies travel or wherein they have made a shifting, settled residence, that the Gypsies have multiplied greatly, and are flourishing in countries such as America, Turkey, Portugal, and parts of Spain and Greece?

The French Gypsies alone have a theory concerning this. They call themselves *Les Hommes du Premier Monde*, and say that Gypsies alone are survivors from the First World, when all men were nomads across salty wastes, all spoke one language, all were brothers. This survival accounts for their peculiar food tastes, the Gypsies alone enjoying herons, hedgehogs, and "wild meat" of all kinds.

In America, where the Gypsies are often very prosperous, especially the New York Gypsies, I think that the general policy of racial tolerance, which is powerful in such places as New York, Chicago, Los Angeles, and San Francisco, which have large, mixed populations, has aided the Gypsy prosperity. A superstitious fear of the traveling people, and a policy of unreasonable intolerance toward them, shames nations and proves to me a deficiency of cultural and spiritual development.

The religion of the Gypsies is a mixture of the local faiths of the countries in which they travel or partly settle, joined with ancient pagan customs of their own. If they are not sun and fire "worshipers," they certainly adore both, and languish without constant contact with them. Hence they suffer and often degenerate in health and character when they live for any lengthy spell in towns.

The Gypsies have their own very peculiar language: Romany Tschib. It links the tribes – even though it is divided into many dialects. Above all it is a secret language: the Gypsies do not like non-Gypsies to know Romany. Romany is described by language experts as being a primeval speech. It is further said that the Gypsy language as it is yet spoken is one of the most ancient in the entire world. Whenever I hear Romany spoken, I hear, in general, the same words. Only the Romany of the Spanish Gypsies differs widely. I was delighted when trying out Romany words on Greek Gypsy children to find that they knew them all!

I think that the Gypsies have succeeded in America because the average American is really a romantic and artistic person. With their modern life mostly being shorn of romance – for which they have to rely on the cinema, theater, or television – when the traveling Gypsy comes by, or the fortune tellers set up their box-like booths of mystery and magic in some drab street-store, the American's heart is kindled and he is pleased to pay for the pleasure of contact with "true romance."

The musical talents of the Gypsies appeal to the Americans, too; and most Gypsies are by nature highly musical. It was as musicians as well as fortune tellers that they were retained at the royal courts in earlier centuries, cherished there for their special talent of reciting and singing old love songs, heroic ballads, and soldiers' songs. The Gypsies themselves mostly manage to avoid military service worldwide. Gypsy troubadours indeed! Lister has this to say:

> A song still haunts me:
> As in the straw I lie,
> Myself still young,
> The world still young,
> And all Provence,
> And its blue sky.

The Gypsies were long considered to be the minstrels and the physicians of Eastern Europe and the Balkans. Their physical beauty and passionate natures, combined with their musical talents, was a love magnet for kings and queens of the many royal palaces where the Gypsies were welcomed and retained. Many Gypsies carry the royal blood of non-Gypsies in their families, although in general they avoid parenting non-Gypsy offspring.

Today Gypsies live in England in the New Forest Compound. (A compound is a place for confining. England's large Gypsy population, forbidden by law from tenting and traveling in their former freedom, are confined there. The compounds are rather less bearable than American Indian reservations.) Gypsy members of the distinguished Wells family, descendants of Caroline and Winifred Wells, who were ladies of Charles II's court (Caroline was with child by him), were granted special land and timber privileges in the New Forest. Shakespeare is believed to have loved a Gypsy girl and to have written his "Dark Lady" sonnets to her. And writers from Cervantes to D.H. Lawrence have been fascinated with the Romanies.

Because of their wonderful memories, the Gypsies were often "keepers of pedigrees" in important families, especially in the Orient, before writing became general. Not only were they keepers of human pedigrees but also of the pedigrees of the horses and dogs of their patrons; through that work they had access to the best horses and hounds of the leading families of Europe.

But the greatest attraction the Gypsies hold the for large mixed population of modern Americans, whatever their racial background, is their occult powers. These powers they divert into hand, sand, and crystal readings; they also use the special Gypsy cards, the ancient Tarot pack.

There is much evidence that playing cards were introduced into Europe by the Gypsies and were then readily taken up by others. Certainly the Gypsies are the keenest of card players, although it is usually the men who play, and the lads. When little boys of other races are playing with marbles, rubber balls, and suchlike, the Gypsy boys of their age are playing intricate card games. It is accepted by all who have studied the history of modern playing cards that before they were put to such uses as pastime and gambling, the different figures and designs had obscure mystical meanings and were employed to carry messages from people to people. The Gypsies are almost the only persons possessing the Tarot pack who can properly interpret them.

The French call the Tarot deck "Le Tarot des Bohemiens" – and Bohemien is their word for Gypsy. The country of origin of the Tarot was believed to be Morocco. At a time in the Dark Ages when all intellectual achievement was suspect and punishable as witchcraft or heresy, wise people from all lands of culture agreed to assemble at one chosen place, probably Morocco, and to formulate a plan to preserve wisdom. Their decision: to create a collection of pictorial symbols to preserve their knowledge. By means of pictorial signs put on cards, they would fool their persecutors, while retaining for themselves the true interpretation of each number and symbol. Therefore it was only a bluff that the Tarot cards were put into the hands of the common people as a game and as a form of fortune telling, for the wise ones alone held the key to their true meanings. In time, to carry this knowledge to their own fraternity of magicians in distant lands, the originators of the Tarot decided to use the Gypsies – the greatest wanderers of the world. They would take the cards and their true meanings with them on their journeys.

But, it is said, the knowledge of the Tarot gave the Gypsies a great new power over the common people. The King Supreme of the Gypsies at that time, observing this new power, commanded his people henceforth to keep the Tarot knowledge secret, sharing this only with the Gypsy race and with no one else! It is further said that that is the reason why, to this day, Gypsies command more powers in magic than any other race. It is known that the Gypsies still teach the Tarot meanings, one generation to the other.

One summer morning, in the Gypsy quarter of Marseilles – Avenue de Corderie, then a crowded collection of shacks and vans, now a fashionable residential place – I well remember coming upon a friend, Teresa Navarro.

The Little Foxes and friend (in plaid); Gypsy quarter, Marseilles

She was sitting out in the sunlight with her many children (known to myself and others who loved them as "The Little Foxes") and instructing them from an odd-looking book, the pages having no written words, only strange symbols, which much resembled those of the Tarot deck. Teresa Navarro was the daughter of that wonderful Algerian Gypsy, Madame Caulas. Called a sorceress by many of the French and Spanish Gypsies who knew her, it was she who had taught me hand-reading.

Teresa was so absorbed in the teaching of her attentive children that at first she was unaware of my presence at her side. Then when she saw me, she closed the book so abruptly, and showed such confusion, it was as if I had caught her in possession of something stolen.

Magicians are in another story about the Tarot cards, a shorter one, which I prefer to the Moroccan one. The magicians of the world agreed to assemble in Alexandria, Egypt, to put into the Great Library there all of their occult knowledge. This fulfilled, a great celebration was held outside the library. In the midst of this celebration came a roaring noise – of flames! The library was on fire, and all their knowledge with it!

Lo, after much discussion, it was decided to give that secret and special information to the world's most traveled, and still traveling, people, the Gypsies. This was duly done.

However, after the passing of time, and the experiencing of the power that came from the Tarot, the Gypsies decided that for the future, the Tarot knowledge would be solely their own. No more sharing.

The Tarot of the Bohemians underwent a change early in the fifteenth century, in Paris. A group of persons interested in the future of playing cards agreed that the suit names of the Tarot should be altered to simpler symbols for gaming. These are still in use today. The cups, as love, became the hearts. The pentacles, which are money, became the diamonds. The wands, for power and growth, became the clubs. And the swords, death and war, became the spades. (In Spanish, *espada* means sword.)

[This is accurate; the previous edition of Juliette's book was incorrect, whether intentionally – as a "Gypsy," Juliette would be likely to hold to the tradition of being confusing, rather than revealing – or not.]

The original Tarot, therefore, went underground – with continuing use by the Gypsies – and the secret societies who were the keepers of the world's occult knowledge went into hiding also.

Some card collectors still possess the old Tarot of the Bohemians, though they are rare. I saw a pack once, in the New Forest [in England], owned by a visitor staying at my friend Olive Wilson's house, and I shall always remember the strange attraction and beauty of those cards! Copies of the Tarot were sold in some New York shops, notably the Hungarian shop of Paprikas Weiss on Second Avenue, and H. Roth and Son on First Avenue, and Chequer on Third Avenue. But these addresses are of long ago, from the first edition of this book, and may not exist any longer. Again, the Tarot is widespread now and can be purchased in a variety of places.

On my travels I have often come across Gypsies using magic or talked with Gypsies concerning magic. One of the best of them all I was to meet in New York.

The Gypsy was Madame Prince, as she called herself. Helena was her first name. Her name must have been other than Prince once, for she was completely un-American both in type and voice. Later she told me that she was Odessa born but had spent most of her life in Hungary and Paris. Her adult life had been in Paris largely, and it was from there that one of her clients had invited her to America. Her patron, a wealthy woman, had died, but she had stayed on and in all probability would live the rest of her life in

America. The American people like the Gypsies. The police here were enemies, as they were to the Gypsies of every land, but she took good care not to have any contact with them and not to give them any reason to visit her apartment.

Her apartment, which I came to know well, was on 14th Street. Although she was a fortune teller (and magician) by profession, she did not have a fortune-telling *ofisa*; she only saw clients by appointment. Her fees began at ten dollars. So she was fortune teller, consultant, and dispenser of magic for the rich.

One interesting quality about Madame Prince was her nostalgia for Hungary. Often when I was with her that nostalgia would come upon her like the sudden attacks of pain that grip heart sufferers. Her region of Hungary had been the Carpathian Mountains, where, she said, before the coming of the Nazis, and then later the Russians, the true Gypsy life had been lived. There the Gypsy men and women had been travelers on horseback, her people rich in horses, riders over the great plains where giant sunflowers grew in golden forests. (Madame Prince was chewing at sunflower seeds, or smoking black paper cigarettes scented with amber, almost every time I visited her.)

The Gypsies of the Carpathian Mountains have fame also for their magnificent bears. Gypsy boy infants were often put to suckle from the she-bears, to gain extra strength and also courage. And to become bonded to the bears for the better training of them to dance and perform in circuses. Oh, the bears: our history so old with them, going back fifty thousand years or more.

And at night, Gypsy singing and dancing around great fires kept away the wolf packs. Hers, Madame Prince's, had been the land of the bear and the wolf, and the acacia blossom. She told me that she would never forget the scent of Hungarian acacia; it brought tears to her eyes to think how much she wanted to be again living in the company of those trees. She often bought jars of acacia-blossom honey from Hungarian shops in New York – only the price of that commodity was so high, she complained, that there should have been pure gold within those jars instead of honey. Inspired by Madame Prince's passion for the acacia tree, I myself bought some jars of acacia-blossom honey from Hungarian shops along Second Avenue. And my children and I enjoyed this, spread thickly on New York's "Monks' Bread," of which I shall tell more.

I first met Madame Prince just off Second Avenue, outside an antique shop on Third Street where my children and I were admiring an exciting collection of amber. All colors were displayed there, many of them very rare. They ranged from pale cream, like ewe's milk, to a peony flower red and charcoal black. A woman dressed all in black, including black silk stockings, was also admiring the amber. I knew she was a Gypsy, although she was short and fat and seemed to have nothing of the Gypsy about her, apart from her magnificent necklace and long hanging earrings of red corals threaded on gold chains. The intense, shining red of the corals made me think that they looked as if they had just been dipped in blood before the wearer had adorned herself.

The woman spoke to me. She had many gold teeth in her mouth; they flashed in the electric lamplight of a New York evening. She asked me what I thought about the amber.

"Beautiful," I replied.

"Not as beautiful as the amber necklace you are wearing," the Gypsy said, pointing to my amber necklace, which had come from Turkey and had been my father's. He was a jewels expert, so likely chose special things for his own use.

In Turkey and many Arabian countries, Oriental men pass tasseled necklaces of beads through their fingers as they talk; it is a form of prayer, or perhaps affectation. Amber or onyx were the most usual for those beads, though in modern times lusterless plastic beads are often used.

"I'm pleased that you like my amber," I told the Gypsy. "It comes from Turkey. And you are wearing magnificent corals," I added.

"I would exchange them with you this very minute! My corals for your amber," the Gypsy said. I am sure that her corals were more valuable than the necklace around my neck. But the necklace had been my father's, as I had said, and he had died tragically in Turkey, and I love him, and would therefore never part with the necklace. I told this to the Gypsy, but she persisted.

"I was born in Odessa; there by the Black Sea is the heart of the amber trade – great lumps of amber are collected along the seashore. I played with the amber lumps as a child. Take my corals! Give me your amber."

"No!" I said with finality. "It is not possible."

We continued to look at the amber displayed in the shop window, and I told the Gypsy the legend about amber being the tears of women, the sisters of the unfortunate Phaeton, who, when Phaeton was overcome by Zeus, were turned into poplar trees, and for ages shed tears for themselves and for their brother: tears of amber. Amber is in truth the resin from forests long ago.

"Amber is a magnet for love," the Gypsy told me, in turn.

My children then began to pull at my arms and whisper to me urgently, "Come away! Come away! She's trying to take your amber necklace. She doesn't look nice."

The Gypsy then said, as if she had heard my children's words, though she could not possibly have done so, "You interest me, and I know you are part Gypsy. Will you visit me soon? Don't delay, come tomorrow, will you? Don't bring the children, do you mind? I've never had any, and they make me nervous – and they stop us from talking."

The Gypsy excited my imagination. I said I would visit her tomorrow. I was delighted she had invited me. She then gave me her card, which said merely, "Madame Helena

Prince of Paris," with her New York address and telephone number. No mention of any fortune telling or similar Gypsy profession, I noticed.

I found Madame Prince's apartment situated above a shop midway along busy 14th Street, down which it is a quite common sight to see the Cadillac cars of the rich New York Gypsies driving by, as they visit the many clothing shops there to buy lengths for the cloth trading in which many of them engage.

When I rang the apartment bell, Madame Prince came to the door wearing a towel over her face, and the partly opened door let out upon me such a cloud of pungent fumes that I was nearly suffocated, and my eyes streamed. Madame Prince laughed at my astonished face and said that she was burning cayenne pepper to change the luck of her apartment, which had not been too good the past month. She was driving away the depression. She was just going out into the street herself, while the pepper burned for a further hour. So would I please visit her apartment the following day, when all the fumes would be out of her place through the windows, and all the depression along with them? Meanwhile, would I accept her invitation to a cafe nearby, where we could drink good coffee, and could talk?

I went along with her, and we drank strong black coffee while Madame Prince enthused over the merits of cayenne pepper. She told me how she used the pepper. Only first she said, "I think you can teach me important things! I thought so when I first saw you. I would teach you also. I want to know what you have learned from my people in other lands for I know we've valuable knowledge. They'd teach you if you lived with them and they liked you. What did you learn? I will teach you the Gypsy things that I know." Therefore I told Madame Prince that I would be happy to do what she suggested, only my Gypsy knowledge was mostly herbal.

She replied that herbal things would interest her very much. She valued that medicine. Her parents in Odessa had used no other. She would "teach herbs" to her clients who came to her for the hand readings.

She began her exchange agreement with me by teaching me about cayenne pepper, which she said was of course a natural plant remedy and was one of the best things that people could use to protect their health and good fortune. I had only given cayenne in treatments for horses and cattle, to ease the pains of colic, and it had been Alsace-Lorraine Gypsies who had taught that to me.

Madame Prince told me to burn dry cayenne pepper on an old tin plate or on the bottom of a reversed tin can. Set this on the fire, or on a gas or electric burner, or the red-hot ashes of a wood fire can be used when outdoors. Start off the burning of the pepper by igniting it with a match. Strong and suffocating fumes will soon begin to arise. The fumes are not harmful to human health [except, do remember not to let the burning fumes get into anyone's eyes, ears, mouth, or genitals], and they possess powers to drive away all evil things: from venomous insects, snakes and rodents, to evil occult influences that cause mental depression, business failures, and that may even influence a person to commit suicide or murder. The fumes will also keep away werewolves, phantoms, and other things of that kind, or drive them away when it is known that they are preying on families. Cayenne pepper is one of the chief things used by the Gypsies of Hungary and Russia when called into homes to remove vampires and other hauntings.

Madame Prince told me further that many times when the cayenne is burning well, the blackened pepper will begin to glow brightly, and then the head of the *bengi* (devil) may appear. If so, it will be seen quite clearly with the horns on either side and colored a bright orange. Orange and blue are the brimstone colors, the devil's favorite colors according to magicians. Did I know that? But I had to tell Madame Prince that orange and blue happened to be my favorite colors also. So I now wondered whose "side" I was on!

The Gypsy laughed heartily. Her voice and laugh were very deep and powerful for a person of such short stature, but both sounded good to my ears and I enjoyed every minute of her company for a long time. (Later I became rather apprehensive.) Her speech, though, was always difficult to understand because her English was dominated by a Bessarabian accent. I preferred it when she spoke in French, as it was easier to understand her then.

I was to tell Madame Prince about some of the medicinal properties of cayenne pepper known to me. A pinch of it in a tablespoon of raw milk is a good remedy in the treatment of common colds and to ease stomach pains. Cayenne pepper is much used in this way by the French Gypsies as a horse medicine. Then herbalists use cayenne pepper to relieve tension in heart attacks. A large pinch of pepper is mixed into honey and swallowed at once. It is at least harmless, unlike many other heart drugs, even if it does not succeed in completely curing the condition. Then cayenne pepper is also valuable when mixed with other herbs to treat parasitical vermin that attack unclean human heads and animal bodies.

We talked about medicinal herbs for a long time, as we had promised, exchanging remedies with one another. I was surprised how much the New-York-living Gypsy knew. As a practicing herbalist, I too had knowledge to impart. But Madame Prince, who did not consider herself an herbalist at all, really out-talked me at our first meeting! I hoped to do better on the next occasion. At least I would be able to help the Gypsy improve the health of her cat, which she told me she loved very much – "as a mother loves an only child."

The cat was supposed to be fading away on account of its poor appetite, and mange had attacked its ears. It bore the strange name of Mesmer, in honor of the eighteenth-century German physician who had popularized mesmerism and whom Madame Prince admired.

As soon as I left the company of Madame Prince I went to a store and purchased a tin of cayenne pepper to take back to my own apartment, to try cayenne pepper for burning as the Gypsy had described to me. I hoped it might drive away any cockroaches that might yet be lingering in the back room, which had – before I had applied my own herbal warfare to compel the speedy removal of their dirty company – formerly been infested with them .

I burned cayenne pepper many times in our apartment. It was possible to shut the door into the front room and thus keep the fumes in the back. Several times a strange glow did appear, and we distinctly saw the devil's head as described by Madame Prince. It became quite a game for my children.

I spent many afternoons of my months in New York sitting at the window of Madame Prince's 14th Street apartment, the Gypsy at my side and her big black cat Mesmer stretched along the windowsill above the steam radiator. Madame Prince was one of the few Gypsies I have met who liked an overheated apartment; only she always showed me the kindness of partly opening a window and turning down the heat while I was visiting her.

We never had any other Gypsies in her apartment. Whereas all the other Gypsy *ofisas* that I knew in New York thronged with Gypsies coming and going, family and old friends, Madame Prince stayed aloof from the New York Gypsy world. She told me that, because she conducted her fortune-telling business differently from the common Gypsy *ofisa*, the other Gypsies were resentful of her. They slandered her and would make trouble for her with the police if she were ever careless enough to give them opportunity to do her harm. She had often seen Gypsies known to her, men and women, walking to and fro along the sidewalk, beneath and in front of her apartment, spying on her. I wondered if Madame Prince was imagining the hostility of other Gypsies towards herself, because all the many times of my visits I never saw any Gypsy near the Prince apartment. And those with whom I spoke concerning Madame Prince had never heard of her.

I had told Madame Prince to feed her cat raw foods, a little raw kosher meat, preferably lamb, for such meat is usually freshly killed and has not been stored for months in refrigeration, with all the vitality of the meat thus lost. For cooked foods, a very little baked fish or lamb. I told her to add some finely chopped fresh herbs – parsley, mint, dill and others – and also to give some whole-grain cereal, such as flaked oats, wheat germ, whole wheat bread, with fresh milk poured over. For the cat's ears, I told her to use very diluted raw lemon juice and a mixture of five powdered herbs, which I gave her. The cat soon showed marked improvement, and the mange disappeared from its ears.

Among the five powdered herbs was rue. This herb, *Ruta*, is well known to all Gypsies, is much used by them, and has special significance for them. One of its uses is against cataract. The yellow flowers of the plant are soaked in water in hot sunlight, until the yellow is extracted into the water; the eyes are then bathed with this many times daily. Concerning rue, the Gypsies claim that not only have they the blessing of Christ because of the help that they gave to him during the time of the crucifixion, they also have the blessing of Mohammed. For when the Arabian prophet was stricken with an illness from which none of his great doctors could save him (likely he had been poisoned; he was dying), a company of ragged Gypsies came to the prophet with a bunch of rue which they urged him to take as a medicine. Mohammed did so, and was speedily cured! To this day the herb rue is known as being sacred to Mohammed, who blessed it and likewise blessed the Gypsies. As a benediction upon the Gypsies, Mohammed promised that the race would be the healthiest and the most fertile of all mankind and would endure forever.

The legends concerning Christ's blessing of the Gypsies are many, though some legends say the Gypsies received a curse, not a blessing, and it is that curse that drives them from country to country, eternal homeless wanderers despised by all others.

The Gypsies tell that when the Romans wanted nails for Christ's cross, a Gypsy blacksmith was ordered to forge the nails. (The principal trade of the Gypsies worldwide was that of metal-smithing. They have claimed that when a former world was destroyed, they came down to earth in sealed vessels of iron, and are therefore the world's oldest people.) The Gypsy smith refused to make any. Another smith, not a Gypsy, was then chosen. So the Gypsy planned to steal the nails from him. He only succeeded in stealing one nail. It was too late then for the non-Gypsy smith to make another, and although the Romans flogged the Gypsy until they nearly killed him, he refused to tell where he had hidden the lost nail. Therefore Christ had His legs held by one nail instead of two on the cross, the feet being nailed together. This in fact made His crucifixion much more painful, as the circulation of blood in His feet was impeded.

Christ, hearing of the Gypsy's suffering on His account, sent for him. From the cross He blessed the Gypsy, and gave the whole Gypsy race a free passport to travel the world and take food and clothing from the other people, but for their real needs only. And they have been doing that ever since!

I have heard two other stories concerning the Gypsies and the crucifixion. One also concerns the nails for Christ's cross. Mary, the Mother, was preparing henna for use on her hair, making herself beautiful for the Passover feast. Her hair was washed and the henna was prepared. Just then a friend hurried to her to tell her that Christ had been taken and was to be crucified. Mary had never imagined that her son would really be taken and she refused to believe her friend, who then pointed out the figure of a Gypsy passing by, and said, "There goes the Gypsy smith taking the nails he has made for Christ's cross." Mary then took up the pot of henna and flung it at the wall, declaring: "As this henna stains the wall forever, so forever, will the Gypsy's race be cursed, to wander the world homeless and despised by all men. They will never be allowed to settle anywhere."

Mary then cursed the henna, saying that henceforth only bad and ugly women would use henna on their hair. The story is of Greek origin, and to this day very few women of Greece henna their hair. Despite the legend, I love henna and often use it. Henna, applied to the head, is a good cure for headache.

The other story concerns a Gypsy woman and a basket of eggs. The woman was taking baked eggs to sell to the crowd who had assembled to follow the crucifixion, waiting to see whether Christ would arise after death as prophesied. One of the crowd, running by, questioned by the Gypsy, said that Christ had risen and had appeared to his disciples and others. The Gypsy would not believe it and exclaimed:

"It is not true! I will not believe it until the eggs that I carry turn from white to red! That is impossible, and this is impossible!" She then heard the people around her crying out, "The eggs! The eggs!" Then, hastily lowering the basket from her head, she found that the eggs were all a vivid red.

This story is of Greek origin, and the holy eggs of Easter, in Greece, are still dyed a bright red. This is supposed to be in memory of the miracle of the Gypsy's basket of eggs. Loaves of bread are baked with a red-shelled egg in the center.

Perhaps because I love – and know – the Gypsies, I believe the first legend: that the Gypsy refused to make the nails for Christ's cross and was blessed. For Gypsies travel because they have hearts of wanderers. Although other people would detain them, make them stay in one place, the Gypsies choose to wander; they are not compelled by others to travel the world. All over the civilized world there are harsh laws directed against all vagrants. But they continue to use the passport that Christ gave to them!

As to making the nails and harming Christ, I think that, more than any other race, the Gypsies are on the side of the persecuted and the hunted. They are traditionally known as shelterers of persons hiding from the law. During the years that Hitler's tyranny was directed against Gypsies and Jews, Gypsies, with their skill at passing illegally from country to country without proper papers, helped many Jews, along with many of their own people, to escape the Nazis.

As for Hitler's persecution of the Gypsies: The Gypsies themselves say that Hitler went to consult a famous Bavarian Gypsy woman fortune teller concerning his chances for further war successes. The Gypsy fortune teller warned Hitler in an urgent way to free all the captive Jews immediately and to cease his murdering of them; otherwise, his evil killings of defenseless innocents would so inspire other countries against him – as was becoming increasingly evident – that he would surely lose the war. If he continued to persecute the Jews he would destroy himself and all his leaders along with the Jews.

What a bold and courageous woman, to speak to Hitler in such a way. Gypsy power! Hitler was surely the most dangerous man in the world at that time, the undisputed leader. It is said to be a true report, and it immediately cost that courageous woman her life. It was also the excuse to commence murdering the Gypsies in all the occupied countries. The police – always in conflict with the law-breaking Gypsies – now could get at them! And likewise at the very desirable Gypsy women and girls. A calamity for the Gypsies.

Hitler stormed at that Gypsy fortune teller, demanding that she change her words, telling her that she had been paid by others to frighten him and so damage the Nazi cause. But she would not take back one word of her warning, saying that she had spoken only what her vision had foreseen. Hitler then, in a rage of anger and fear, left the Gypsy and said he would immediately have her put to death as a traitor to the Reich, and that he would have put to death along with her every Gypsy in German-occupied territory.

"Round them up and send them to the gassing places. Rat poisoning for the rats," he had stormed.

So the deportation and gassing of the Gypsies of Germany, Poland, Hungary, France, Greece, and elsewhere began, with thousands, including women and children, taken. The whole race was classified by the Nazis as "social undesirables" and listed for total extermination. It is said also that Hitler considered that the Gypsies might be one of the Lost Tribes of Israel.

T. Geve, in his tragic book on the Nazi death camps entitled *Youth in Chains*, says of the swoop of the Gestapo upon Berlin's unsuspecting Gypsy population: "German Gypsies could find no explanation for this sudden stab in the back. Whereas the arresting of the German Jews meant that . . . the threats of ten years ago had materialized." Geve also describes the Gypsies in Auschwitz, especially the Gypsy boys – for he himself had been a German Jewish boy in that terrible place. With "Z" for *Zigeuner* branded on their arms, the Gypsies had been made public entertainers to the camp officials and visitors, who enjoyed the sentimental Romany songs and their seductive dances.

Himmler, one of the foremost Nazi leaders, was, of them all, the one to take the greatest interest in the Gypsies. He found them "highly entertaining" and visited Auschwitz – that being the principal camp for their extermination – regularly to stare at them.

Their wild hairstyles, outlandish clothes, their special talents for song, music, and dance, all allured him. Yet he had no pity for them, nor for anyone. He knew that they were ever on a procession to the gas chambers, and that made an enjoyable change of faces for him.

There was always plenty of new material; they exterminated one group when a change of faces was considered desirable to prevent boredom of the spectators. Then a new group was led onto the camp stage.

Dancing group in traditional clothes;
note dwarf in front with rose; Granada

The Gypsies also entertained other prisoners with clairvoyant sessions. It is said of the Gypsies in the death camps that again and again they foretold the times of the gassings and knew who would be taken and who would be spared; and they could foretell their own death times.

A Gypsy boy who was unable to foretell the future is described by T. Geve in the last pages of his book. The imminent capture of Auschwitz by the Allies had caused the removal of many of the captives to Buchenwald. Buchenwald, too, was soon threatened with capture by the Allies, and the prisoners were huddled near the gates, wondering whether they should join the camp transports leaving the emptying camp or hide themselves and stay behind. Among the columns of silent, worried-looking camp inmates on their way to the gate, there was a sunburnt Gypsy lad, a recently taken prisoner at Buchenwald. He seemed only confident as he strolled along, and he called to T. Geve and to the other hesitant men alongside Geve: "What are you waiting for? Come along with me. I am a Gypsy and glad to be out here in the open air where the birds sing. It's good to belong to the countryside. Farewell, comrades, I am off to freedom."

All those who left in the last columns from Buchenwald were killed; and the Gypsy must have died along with them.

Survivors of the Auschwitz death camp, including Benjamin Babiker, a Hungarian, and Laura Tepper, a Romanian, remember the strange and terrible night when a crowd of several thousand Gypsies – foretelling their own deaths by gassing on the following day – put out all the lights in their prison and filled the night with unearthly singing and screaming. Those two witnesses and informants, knowing my love for the Gypsies, wanted to share with me what they had witnessed, so that it would not be forgotten. I shall never forget the horror and the pathos in their reports to me. Never! Never!

At Auschwitz the Gypsies were housed apart from the other inmates in a special building comprising blocks A, B, and C. It was known as the *Zigeuner Lager*, and also "The Gypsy Road to Death." Because of the known violent Gypsy attempts at escape in all the camps where they were imprisoned, the Auschwitz Gypsy unit was a vast steel cage very close to the gas chambers. On that particular night, knowing they could not escape, the Gypsies not only filled the place with their terrible mourning, they also staged a final Gypsy rebellion: they wrecked the interior of their cage.

When the guards came on the following morning to drive the Gypsies into the gas chambers – just as the Gypsies had foreseen – they were amazed at the shambles that they found there in the Gypsy quarters. They consulted together whether they should subject the Gypsies, in punishment for their rebellious behavior, to a death more cruel than gassing. But, meanwhile, the Gypsies had advanced towards the guards in such a hissing, cursing, gesticulating mob, toddlers and old grannies all joining in the chorus of screaming hate and protest, that the guards had to retreat and bring back well-armed reinforcements, which included the well-trained camp dogs, fed on human flesh so that they would be good at their work of attacking human beings – as they were. Horrendous, indeed.

Again, the Gypsies howled their wrath and cursed the Nazi regime; some Gypsies were spitting blood in their frenzy. The guards, frightened by the curses shouted at them, were thankful when all the Gypsies had been driven into the gas chamber and into oblivion: condemned to unjust death by Gypsy haters. On the day and night of July 31st into August 1st, 1947, driven forward by biting wolf-dogs, whips, and revolvers, nearly 4,000 Gypsies were "destroyed" by gassing.

A pathetic, but to be remembered, item of the gassings was the fact that the Gypsies knew that, closed up in the chamber, when the poison gas was turned on and began to fill their lungs, everyone would make an uncontrollable rush towards the sealed door. The old folk would be the first to be knocked down and trampled. Therefore, the Gypsies arranged that their old people should stay at the back of the chamber so as not to be painfully crushed. And that was found to be the case. The old folk died, of course, but not trampled in a more painful death then that of gassing. Parents lay upon their children and helped them. All was carefully arranged.

Another true story of care for the aged was told to me, a Jewish one this time. A Jewish Hungarian grandmother was purchased for, literally, a trunkful of gold from a German concentration camp. The payment was arranged through Switzerland. The trunk of gold pieces was delivered to the camp yard and the very aged grandmother set free.

In an uncanny way, using their so-called second sight, their famed seeing into the future, as possessed by biblical characters, the Gypsies would know beforehand who was next to be forced into the gas chambers. Through the steel wire mesh of their heavily fortified enclosure (because it was difficult to get the Gypsies into them – they had managed to overcome and strangle several of the guards), they managed to speak with non-Gypsies, telling them how they carefully planned to protect the aged and the children from the pain of trampling.

They also implored the camp people to spread the Gypsy dead with garlic, to keep off the Auschwitz rat hordes, which were known (and seen) to eat human bodies when the flesh was still warm, and even still had some movement. The arrival of two huge trucks filled with garlic, and marked *Zigeuner Lager*, was remembered at Auschwitz. None knew from where that garlic had come. The truck drivers were Gypsies. Both were arrested and surely killed, for both simply disappeared.

I love the poem, "By the Gypsies' Graves" by Hungarian Karoly Bari (translated by Laura Schiff):

> Roots pound the chambers of their hearts,
> A silver veil of snailspit glistens on their faces.
> They left the world, unnoticed.
> From their sinewy arms twisted trees grow.
> They walk on stars – in shoes.

Gypsy shoes are boots! I remember those boots of the Hungarian Gypsies in the Evesham camp, but mostly they are a barefoot people. I remember the horse-trader Gypsies of the Westmoreland border in England, coming down into the Yorkshire dales with their teams of horses, barefoot people despite the weather turned cold. But it was his boots that helped to mark the pied Piper of Hamelin as being a Gypsy: "His cloak of many colors" and his high boots with long thongs bound around the legs, "the same as Gypsies wear."

One Gypsy child who escaped from a German concentration camp was Joe Pischlech. I heard his story in New York from our friend Jess Aland, who worked in the United Nations there. Jess had previously worked in important refugee organizations in Europe, especially in Germany after World War II. There, in a German refugee orphanage, Jess met Joe, who was awaiting American adoption. Both of his parents had been killed; in the camp where Joe had been found, he was a solitary Gypsy survivor.

Jess went to the orphanage to invite one of the children to spend the Christmas holidays with her. Lucky is the child who spends Christmas with Jess! Mine came to know her in New York around Christmastide, and she took them into the enchanted world of New York's children's pantomimes, ballet, and puppet shows, in Greenwich Village and nearby.

The orphanage asked her to take the only Gypsy boy in the place because he seemed miserably unhappy and would not mix with the other children. The only information they had concerning him was: "Gypsy. Roman

Catholic (from the way he said his prayers). Both parents and all relatives, killed."

Jess told me that she would never forget her Christmas guest. Aged possibly eight years, deathly white of face, he was dressed up in strange finery that the other children had lent him for the occasion of his holiday outside the orphanage. She remembered especially, of his clothing, chartreuse-colored woolen gloves, so large that they were tied on with tape, and the yellowish-green gloves clashed with the pink woolen scarf knotted around his thin neck. Clothing was very scarce in Germany at that time, but Jess took her guest to a Jewish family she knew who had many children, and they fitted out the Gypsy in quieter-colored and more comfortable clothes.

The boy was not silent and unfriendly as reported to Jess by the wardens of the orphanage. He proved to be both resourceful and friendly. His first words of greeting to her had been, "Thank you! Let's get out of here!" And the boy went with determination to the door.

The Gypsy had greeted with ecstasy every snow-covered fir tree they had passed on the way to the country hotel where Jess was taking her guest. "Christ trees," he called them. She heard the child moving restlessly in the hotel bed, which she had had made up alongside her own. When she asked him why he could not sleep, he told her that he was cold. "Couldn't we sleep all in one bed as my people sleep?" So Jess lifted the Gypsy into her bed, and he was asleep within moments.

Joe was normal in every way, untouched by his experience in the concentration camp, except for one derangement concerning meat. If the child set eyes upon any meat in a shop or on the table or even shredded in stews, at sight of the slightest particle of meat in any form, he would lose all color from his face, his eyes would widen unnaturally, and he would have a fit of uncontrollable trembling. Sometimes he would faint away. And always he would be crying out in German: "Flesh, flesh!"

He would never explain the reason for his terror but would press his hand over his mouth to keep back speech, apparently not wanting to remember and be frightened further by any memory of some unspeakable horror that he must have witnessed in the camp. Perhaps the big dogs kept at the camps tore some Gypsies to pieces, for it is known that this had been one of the pastimes of the perverted Nazi rulers of some concentration camps. Or perhaps he had seen cannibalism in the camp when human beings were made abnormal by hunger as stated at the Eichmann trial.

Jess formed a deep friendship with the Gypsy boy. Then came the time for his adoption. Joe Pischlech was going to America, to a Roman Catholic family in New York, far from the forests, of course, and the "Christ trees" growing there. The tragic part of the adoption, for Jess, was that the orphanage told her she would have to sever all relationship with the boy, as the adoption society did not want any past associations to enter the new lives that the children would be beginning in New York. That way, in the matter of Joe Pischlech, he might be cured of his meat obsession.

Suddenly, at the airport, at the commencement of the journey to America, Joe refused to leave with the other children. With true Gypsy determination he said that he had changed his mind about America, and would be staying with Jess! So Jess was sent for. She had to tell a lie to the boy, for he would never have entered the plane otherwise. She felt, with the authorities, that the Gypsy child would be happier far away from Germany. "Find a house for us," she said, "and I'll join you as soon as I finish my work here."

"Right," said Joe, "work hard, for I'll send for you very soon."

That was years ago. Jess is now in New York herself. She looks carefully at any dark children she sees anywhere who seem to be about what Joe's age would be by now. She would like to find him again to make sure that he is happy.

Only could any child ever be happy again after the terror and the starvation that Joe Pischlech, and the unnumbered crowds of fellow Gypsy and Jewish children, suffered in the Nazi camps?

In all the world's ugly history of racial hatred, never before has such unspeakable cruelty been recorded. The driving of screaming, fear-demented children into the stinking gas chambers, each child's terror adding to its neighbor's, little brothers leading little sisters by the hand, older children carrying the babies. It is estimated that six million persons perished in the Nazi gas chambers in World War II. There was a mass gassing of 4,000 Jewish French children, mostly from Paris, and 3,000 Hungarian Gypsy children. Although that terrible tragedy of the organized, scientific, and merciless murder of millions of civilians happened so many years ago, I believe that the screams of the Jewish and Gypsy children can still be heard lingering on in the winds when they blow from the direction of those countries in which the Nazis established their death camps. The human race will never recover from the shame of those fiendish crimes. I would feel more proud if I were a sparrow or a wood louse.

Hitler was aware of the occult powers of the Gypsies, and he had been told how they fought when forced into the gas chambers. He would have liked to have withdrawn his death order from them, but he had not the courage to do so. He knew that the world would decide that he was afraid of the Gypsies and he would lose his supreme reputation. So he dared not revoke his Gypsy extermination order.

Afraid, haunted, doddery, he gave himself up to addicition: to the evil-smelling root of the herb valerian. He figuratively disappeared in the vapors of that strange plant whose flowers are composed of myriads of tiny red crosses.

Valerian has pretty pink or red flowers. Taken in over-large doses, as Hitler used it, it will cause hallucinations. But with carefully controlled use, it is nerve soothing and a good treatment for shock. I have used it often to soothe shocked animals.

The Gypsies claim that they won World War II; they overcame Hitler with their occult powers. Thunderous because of what Hitler had done to their people, especially to their children, they spirited him away clouded in valerian fumes. Hitler so totally vanished that not even his valerian-stained teeth were to be found.

There should be a great "thank you" from the world to the Gypsy people. Unlike other peoples, they have received little compensation for what they suffered from Hitler and his Nazis. The Jews, to some extent, obtained financial compensation. The Gypsy claims were mostly ignored.

What the eyes may see can terrify the human mind. The Gypsies know this well, and in their dealings with magic they may make use of this. The notorious among the Gypsy fortune tellers, especially in New York, will sometimes make use of a devil's head to frighten victims into parting with money, sometimes considerable sums of money being extorted in this way. But I can say truthfully that such trickery is rare, and the tally of Gypsy crimes of that sort must be as low as one in several thousand, compared to the vast amount of thievery and general trickery that goes on in New York every hour of every day. Nearly every friend of mine in New York at one time or another has lost money or property to thieves, and in no case were Gypsies involved! A friend of a friend was induced to part with ten dollars against his will, to a New York Gypsy fortune teller, but that was his own folly.

These ugly little devils' heads can be purchased in shops in Mexico and South America. I have seen them there in curio shops. They are usually carved out of white wood, sometimes of ivory, which makes them look more realistic. They are tiny things, usually the size of a small walnut. They have a grinning, evil-looking expression, and have black human or horse hair glued on. On either side of the head is a sharp horn. The Gypsies prick their victims with these horns during the rite of frightening money away from a victim. During this rite, a raw egg white is often poured over the devil's head to give it an added horror: It is slimy and apparently moving.

A friend once parted with fifty dollars in such a rite. She was a well-educated person with a university degree, not an ignorant person in any way! The Gypsy promised to change her financial luck with the use of a big piece of money (she had asked for a hundred-dollar bill, but R.B. did not have one in the house, fortunately). The fifty-dollar bill was put into a stained scarf, together with several tomatoes, and suddenly a devil's head appeared, red from the tomato juice and squirming among the mess. The fifty-dollar bill disappeared – a few shreds of paper that looked like the money were all that was left. The Gypsy said that the devil had gotten in and spoiled the money-making process for her. The money was ruined! She was sorry, but that sometimes happened when the client was doubting the Gypsy's ability to work well for her. Sickened by the whole thing, the horrible image of the leering, bloody devil's head still in her mind, R.B. was thankful to let the money maker go out of her sight and would rather forfeit the money than have a further minute of that Gypsy's company. So the devil's head is sometimes used.

The use of a devil's head was mentioned in a long article on Gypsy trickery entitled "The Beautiful Flower" published in the *New Yorker* some years ago. The Gypsies still smart from this article, written by an ex-policeman in charge of Gypsy affairs in New York. They often mentioned the article to me, protesting:

"The *gendarmi* (police) made us all bad; we are not all bad, as you know who have been with us in many countries. We have the bad among us, as do all races, but we do no more ill than other races; we think we do less, because we want less than the others."

That statement seemed to embody much truth to me. In all my dealings with the Gypsies, they have never deprived me of anything, neither money nor property. Sometimes in the past, until I came to know horses better, they sold me bad horses, but that is all. They have helped me and befriended me wherever I have known them. During the most difficult time of my life, when I had typhus and was alone in a Spanish watermill with my two young children, the Gypsies definitely saved us, together with my own faith in natural medicine. A Spanish Gypsy girl, Rosario Heredia, fostered my two-month-old baby daughter, Luz, feeding her at her breast along with her own son, born nearly at the same time. Also, the Gypsies taught me their herbal medicine, and the knowledge helped to save me during the typhus.

As for centuries the Gypsy people have traveled the world in a state of poverty, they have needed to beg for their simple enough needs as any wandering monk has to beg. Gypsies have often been refused even a drink of water by non-Gypsies. Therefore, when not given the little they need, they take, as all nomads must take from the land as they travel from one destination to another. The Gypsies have trained themselves to be satisfied with very spare rations. When Gypsies have been invited to dine with me, their appetites have been birdlike, making my children and me feel greedy by comparison – although I think we eat far less than the average, for we eat mostly raw vegetables or fruits [and goat cheese, bread and honey].

Many of the town-frequenting Gypsies of America now send their children to school, at least long enough for them to learn to read and write, and their children can read the slander against them found in the American press. They are hurt by this and made ashamed of their Gypsy race. Caterina Markovitch showed me an article from the *Los Angeles Times*, published just before Christmas 1960, the season of "goodwill to all mankind." Judging from the finger-marked and crumpled state of the newspaper clipping, it had been much passed around among Gypsy families. It read:

> GYP MAKES IT WARY CHRISTMAS (New York. U.P) Watch out for the gypsy artists and petty thieves. If you don't, they'll get your money, returning nothing for something. The no-overhead profiteers, including pickpockets, come out of the woodwork in record numbers during the crush before the holiday. The president of the National Better Business Bureau said in an interview: "Because shoppers aren't wary, hundreds of millions of dollars reach the hands of gypsters during the holiday shopping spree."

The world has long slandered the Gypsies, and there has never been a lawyer to defend them. In England, the Gypsy Lore Society, from its headquarters at Liverpool University (which I attended for several years), watches over the interests of the Gypsies. Until his death, the famous portrait painter Augustus John, who lived much with the Gypsies, was president. Dora Yates, M.A., author and Gypsy authority, was the secretary for many years.

The Gypsies have often been accused of such slanderous things as eating their parents, eating cats and rats, poisoning wells, causing cattle plagues, causing crops to fail, and above all, stealing children.

To this very day, in England, when a child is reported missing, the Gypsy encampments are searched. As the Gypsies have such a keen racial pride, it is most unlikely that they would desire to bring up among themselves any child not of their own *kawlo rat* (black blood). That same pride in blood accounts for the fact that marriages outside the race are still rare, more rare than among the orthodox Jews, for instance, who still traditionally go into full mourning when a son or daughter marries outside the Jewish faith.

There is an herb, with whorls of small-lipped, whitish flowers, called Gypsywort [*Lycopus europaens*, formerly of the Labiate family, now the Lamiaceae family]. It grows in damp places and yields a dark juice which stains cloth a permanent black. Supposedly the Gypsies use it to stain dark the white skin of non-Gypsy children that they have stolen. From this reputation, the French call it *Herbe des Bohemiens.*

The only true case I know of in which Gypsies took a non-Gypsy child, was told to me in New York by Bee Bogen. She herself was stolen by the Gypsies as a small child. She is now a grown woman and a noted astrologer.

I feel sure that the Gypsies recognized her occult talents when they chose to take her from a Florida orange grove where she had been playing, in the charge of a maid. They had probably hoped to use the talents of the child later in the Gypsy fortune-telling profession. Anyway, this true story ended well. Bee Bogen's mother was in the hospital at the time. She had lost a child many years younger than Bee, who was born to her late in life. With the loss of Bee, also, she was left childless and inconsolable. The Gypsies kept Bee with them for some months, then, hearing of the great grief of the mother, put the child back one day, in the orange grove from which they had taken her, and sent a message to the mother that her child was awaiting her. They told her that her child was special, and that they hoped she understood this.

My own child Luz is supposed to have a typical Gypsy face; maybe her foster mother – Rosario Heredia – influenced this. Though again, after her, she was fostered by a Spanish goat.

The Spanish Gypsies of the Sierra Nevada above Granada always gave Luz the title "Luz España." Never the Luz without the España. That was her title and it was heart-touching to hear it. It was her baby bravery in surviving so many hazards. Firstly, the uncaring miller's wife who spoon-fed her with goat's milk only when she had time, or remembered to do so during my bout with typhus. Luz was a little skeleton when the Gypsy Rosario offered her breast milk. Then came her fostering by a nanny goat, and her suckling from the goat's udder – memorable to witness. [For the full tale, read *Spanish Mountain Life*, available from Ash Tree Publishing.]

An American friend, Sonje Siegmann, originally from Denmark where the Gypsies are still called Tartars, gave Luz a pair of pure gold, half-moon earrings because she looks so much a Gypsy. The earrings have a romantic history associated with the Danish Gypsies. They came into the family through Sonje's aunt, Selene. Some traveling Gypsy smiths visited the big house of Aunt Selene's parents to mend the family metalware. They camped out in the grounds for several days. In their party was a young Gypsy man of great beauty. Aunt Selene ran away with him, returning to the forests with that Gypsy family of smiths. She lived with the Tartars for two years, until, as is very usual in such cases of mixed marriage, Gypsy with non-Gypsy, the animosity of the other Gypsy women drove her away. She returned home, bringing with her a baby son, and in her ears the Tartar golden earrings.

I could not bear the thought of my child losing one of those earrings of such special Gypsy history, and therefore every night as Luz slept, I touched her earrings to make sure that the clasps were secure, through the ear holes, so the earrings would not fall out on the following day and be lost.

Gypsy jewelry is always interesting and is often symbolic. My friend Madame Prince of 14th Street knew much about this. About the powers possessed by jewels, and how they are influenced by those who have possessed them formerly. That is why the jewelry of Gypsies is usually buried with them. That is perhaps why she wanted my amber necklace, which my adventurous Gypsy-like father had formerly carried around the world with him.

Madame Prince always wore the same jewels herself: fine corals of a dark red color. A treble row coral necklace, and from her ears, short gold chains holding rows of matching corals. The dark red of her jewelry looked well against her sallow skin. Under electric light her corals glowed strangely.

The Gypsy told me that red corals are known to be under the strong influence of the sun, and that they have the powers to keep away melancholy and misfortune from those who wear them. Light coral is entirely different, as it is powerfully influenced by the moon and is known to attract melancholy. Light corals, therefore, are never worn by Gypsy women, who are really Queens of the Corals, because the Gypsy race have been collecting fine corals ever since coral was first found and used for adornment.

Madame Prince crossed herself and touched her corals as she informed me that all phantoms and all monsters of the nether world, including vampires, are afraid of dark corals as dogs are afraid of whips – as the Gypsies know.

She told me a strange recipe for a red amulet which featured dark corals, and was to be worn around the neck, whether person or horse, and was long famed in the protection that it gave to the wearer against many things, including evil astral influences, evil powers of magicians or sorcerers, vampires, venomous serpents and other poisons. The amulet also had the power to draw out from the body all kinds of poisons, whether of disease or from outside sources. The amulet was reputed to be able to absorb completely all that is harmful.

This was the invention, or the discovery from the many magicians with whom he had consorted, of the great medieval doctor, herbalist and magician himself, Theophrastus Paracelsus von Hohenheim, to this day known to the fortune-tellers of the world and honored by them as one of the greatest of all the magicians.

The recipe which I was shown was set down in very fine handwriting, and I was surprised to know that it was Madame Prince's own. She wrote some further lines in front of me, in the same hand, to prove this!

The Paracelsus recipe reads: [Caution: Do not follow.]

> Take eighteen freshly-killed toads, sun-dry them and pound them into a fine powder. Take note that the drying of the toads be very speedy in order to prevent putrefaction. Add to the powdered toads a number of blood-soaked cloths, the cloths to be cut into fine shreds. To all this add half a drachm each of red corals, pieces of jasper and smaragda [Greek for emerald]; then one drachm of seed pearls, and three drachms each of the roots of the plants *Tormentilla erecta* [now *Potentilla erecta*] and *Dictamus albus* [dittany or burning bush]; of Oriental saffron forty grams [very expensive], half an ounce each of white arsenic [poison] and auro-pigment, a few grains each of musk and amber. Grind all down to a fine powder [breathing the dust

> is poisonous] and mix well together. Then make a paste of the mixture, using rose-water and gum tragacanth when the moon is in the sign of the scorpion.

It is agreed that the most potent time for magic forces is during that period each year between October 23rd and November 23rd when the sun and moon are together in the sign of Scorpio, and especially at the new moon. As I was born in the midst of all this magic, under the sign of Scorpio, on November 11th, on the eleventh hour of the eleventh day of the eleventh month, it might account for my having that Gypsy talent of reading hands! The Gypsies believe so.

The paste is then to be formed in tablets weighing from one to two ounces each, or more, dependent upon the size of the wearer. The tablets are to be hardened by drying, and then wrapped individually in red silk cloth. The completed amulet is sewn onto a cord, ready for wearing.

Madame Prince told me that the Gypsies sold those amulets by the thousands in Hungary and in the near Balkan countries, and they were always very scrupulous about keeping to the exact recipe of Paracelsus. They would often use for the blood-soaked cloths, menstrual ones, believing that they held the most potent powers.

Although in this age of scientific reason, when things of the realm of magic are described and dismissed as superstitious and ridiculous, and one always hears that Gypsy fortune-tellers are finished and have no place in modern life, the true fact is that the Gypsy fortune-telling places, whether tent, van, or a commercial New York *ofisa*, draw crowds of clients. The Gypsy people brought fortune-telling and magic with them from the unknown mysterious country of their origin, possibly from the East, cradle of the occult and the mysterious, and the Gypsy women remain the priestesses of the cult of magic.

Madame Prince knew much about the making of Gypsy amulets, love potions, and other things of the kind.

She considered that the flower with the greatest power to attract love is that cool, white, and intensely fragrant thing, which hides in dark places in woods and forests, the lily-of-the-valley. This is why brides, though usually unaware of the reason, like to carry bouquets of that flower on their wedding day. Lily-of-the-valley is a springtime flower and spring is a favored time for weddings. When persons have met with ghosts and afterwards have tried to describe their encounter, many of them have told of a sweet scent – "like lily-of-the-valley" – being present with the ghost.

When a childhood friend whom I had loved deeply, and who was killed in World War II, came to me in a dream soon after his death, and came so clearly that I was able to reach out my hands and touch him – for he was more than a phantom – I was aware for many hours after he had left me of the lingering and powerful scent of lily-of-the-valley filling my room. At that time I didn't know that flower was associated with spirits of the dead.

As an herbalist, I know that the flower spikes and the leaves of lily-of-the-valley, made into a brew and taken with honey, are a proved medicine for the human heart, being both a powerful tonic and healer. [Caution: Can be poisonous.]

Orange blossom is also worn by brides, with real reason, for it entraps and holds love. Lemon blossom possesses yet greater love powers. Paracelsus recommended the balm plant – *Melissa* – to bring love and to delay the coming of

old age. To return to the lemon tree: its flowers are, above all other flowers, my favorite. And it fascinates me that it belongs to the plant family named for rue (the herb of Grace): the *Rutaceae*, or citrus family. Lemons, and their blossoms, possess the deep healing and magic of the rue plant itself.

Through the centuries, strange things have been used in magic. Madame Prince told me that needles and pins (small and large), big nails, brush bristles, hairs of horses and hogs, slivers of glass, the extracted teeth of wolves and other animals, hen and cockerel beaks, and many other strange things have all been cut or magnetized out from victims held in the powers of evil magicians. A Gypsy skilled in beneficial magic would be sent for by the relatives of the afflicted person, and after drawing out the foreign body from the victim, she would embed the object in the body of a tree, choosing for preference an elder, oak, or hawthorn for such a rite, the article being fixed into the tree bark on the side that would be touched by the light of the rising sun, and from there the thing would work like a magnet, to draw to itself the power of evil that the magician put into the body of the victim when inserting the pin, nail, tooth, or other foreign object. The patient treated by the Gypsy would speedily recover once the evil had been magnetized away. Madame Prince had seen this done often. She had once seen a large coal cinder removed from the breast of a young woman, caused to be put there by the husband's sister, who was jealous of the woman.

Warts, to this day, are cured by Gypsy treatments. One treatment that makes use of slugs is often described in writings concerning Gypsy medicine. The slug is killed and then rubbed over whichever part of the person – the face, the hands, other parts – are afflicted with warts. The slug is then thanked and nailed to a tree nearest to the person's home: again the tree used is preferably elder, oak or hawthorn. As the slug's body withers, so likewise the warts of the person being treated are supposed to shrivel and disappear.

It is unlikely that a true Gypsy would use a snail, as is sometimes employed in wart treatment, as snails are looked upon with much affection by Gypsies, who say of them that they, like the Gypsies, go around the world carrying their houses on their backs, as the Gypsies once traveled and travel yet in many countries – with their tents strapped to their backs.

Gypsies still make little wax figures in the image of sick persons, male or female. They make them to cure victims of bad magicians or victims of other baleful occult forces. Nails or big needles or pins are then driven into the wax figures, especially through their heads or genital regions, and the sick person in whose image they have been made is in that way cured of fevers, epilepsy, apoplexy, general paralysis, blindness, and other afflictions.

In Manzanillo, the tropical Mexican port, my children and I dug out from the cliff-sides nearly twenty wonderfully-made clay images. They were household images of about two thousand years ago, certainly pre-Columbian. They were used to protect the home from evil spirits. Some of the faces had been made to look very ugly, with squinting expressions, or with eyes looking in both directions – double eyes – to frighten away baleful things.

Wax images of a different kind are used by lovesick people being helped by the Gypsies. Made in the shape of a man or a woman, and marked with the initials of the desired person, they are bound around with sprigs of thyme or rosemary, then kept under the pillow of the one wanting to win a wife, a husband, or merely a lover, to attract to their side the object of their love. For this purpose, the New York Gypsies made little images from pink-tinted candle-wax and used chips of sandalwood to anoint them. I have seen some charming Gypsy wax figures, too finely made to be squashed under pillows!

The *botanicas*, herbal stores, in New York's Spanish Harlem, sell magic potions. Some are of Gypsy origin, some are not. And Kiehl's Pharmacy, still at 109 Third Avenue in Manhattan, advertised love potions.

Madame Prince once showed me a table drawer filled with worthless things in which she nevertheless took pride because, so she told me, she had charmed them away from their owners against their will. There were locks of hair and tawdry trinkets – perhaps the good ones, if there had ever been any, had already been sold. There were hair combs with the grease and hair still adhering to them, fans and nail scissors and such old-fashioned things as men's monocles.

She said that she kept them to remind herself of her powers, adding that she had never done anyone any harm; and she had done many persons much good. I believed such a declaration, as she was so kind to Mesmer, her cat, and to the sparrows and pigeons that came to her windows in great numbers. There, on the sills, she put more than the usual stale bread leavings offered to city birds. She purchased sunflower seeds, mixed bird seed, shredded coconut, suet, raisins, flaked oats – she even cooked rice for them, a real banquet – and she offered her feelings of love for them, too.

Madame Prince told me a story that well illustrates the cleverness of pigeons. Some other birds are equally intelligent, including poultry. One lunchtime Madame Prince was to dine out and was late for her appointment. The insistent tapping of pigeon beaks on her windowpanes reminded her that she had not fed the birds. But her windows were blocked by piled snow, and she did not have time to clear them then. Therefore she decided to feed the birds when she returned. She next heard a rapping on her door – she was not expecting callers. When she opened the door, three pigeons flew in – they had been the knockers! Of all the many doors in the apartment house, the pigeons, having gained entry into the building somehow, had found hers.

Madame Prince decided to clear her window of snow and put out food for the birds: she was so touched by the cleverness of the pigeons that she preferred to be very late for her appointment and annoy her friends rather than keep the birds waiting any longer for their meal!

But good companion that Madame Prince was to me, and kind as she was, I began to feel that she was using her formidable powers to charm my amber necklace from me! She was forever touching it and sighing over it, saying that she preferred such amber even to dark corals. However, I too possessed some power, and feeling the compelling, magnetic eyes of Madame Prince upon me, I would remind myself of my birth under Scorpio, the very sign that she herself had told me was supreme in magic, whereas Madame Prince herself was only under the sign of Cancer – of some potency in magic but not to be compared to Scorpio!

I never quarreled with Madame Prince, only my friendship with her waned as she became imperious and demanding, reprimanding me when I failed to visit her daily. I had become acquainted with many other Gypsies in New York by then, many of them with interesting, beautiful daughters and sons, and like most Gypsies they were generous and entertaining and never demanding in the way of Madame Prince.

I went to make my good-byes to Madame Prince before I left for Mexico, and I took her a gift of a colorful pure silk Spanish scarf that someone had once given me but that I had never worn. The gift pleased her very much, and she took me with her to a nearby shop and bought for me, and to take back to my two children, pretty red heart-shaped candy boxes filled with sugared almonds – it being near to Valentine's Day when we were leaving New York, and such things were being sold in most of the confectionary shops.

On my return from Mexico, I made an early visit to Madame Prince, but true to the Gypsy way, especially in

New York, she had gone elsewhere already, and her apartment was occupied by others. No New York Gypsy seemed friendly with her, no one could tell me where she had gone. Only I was able to learn from a friendly woman in that same building on 14th Street that the Gypsy had gone away because of personal sorrow. Her cat had run out from her apartment and had been hit by a car and killed. Madame Prince, consumed with grief for her cat, had left almost at once. It is again typical of Gypsies who believe that one should not sigh, because with every sigh some of the life force escapes from the human body. Also they say that tears shed for the dead scorch the souls of the dead; there should be demonstrations of love and praise, but no weeping.

Cats in the center of New York are seldom let out to have freedom in the streets. They get cat litter put into a box in their owner's apartment and are taught to use that for their excrement. That seems to work very well, but it does not offer a fully happy nor healthy life for any cat. However, I have met long-lived and happy indoor cats.

Madame Prince's cat had always been confined to her apartment where she lavished upon him the affection that a woman shows to a man or to her children. Madame Prince had once shown me a photograph of her Bessarabian Gypsy husband: an undistinguished face notable only for his merry eyes and the big mustache with waxed and tightly curled ends. The Gypsy had told me that her husband had been a mere knife-grinder when she had first met him in Hungary, although like herself, he had been Odessa-born.

Attracted by a person from her own birthplace and seeing the possibilities for success present in the man, she had willed him to marry her, using the wax figures she had told me about as part of a lesson from her on magic. Once married to her, he had prospered, and in time had become sharpener of hunting knives and swords to the greatest families in Hungary and Russia, including royalty. He never gave her children, but he gave other women children, and when she had passed beyond the age of childbearing, she – in bitterness – left him and went to Paris, finally settling in America.

In time I gave up looking for Madame Prince or asking the other New York Gypsies if they knew her. Only I remembered the magic that she had taught me. I wish she had taught me how to employ magic to turn an empty purse into a full one!

My friend Madame Prince and my father's amber necklace. Where is it, then? I had forgotten all about it until revising this book. For years I wore a necklace given to me by a Bedouin Arab in Israel. This beautiful Bedouin necklace is a leather thong onto which are threaded triangular pieces of leather studded with brass to make various designs. One is a heart. Big, blue beads of glass – typically Arab – cover the leather thong and are threaded into it. I love that necklace, and it keeps me warm in cold weather. I have thus not thought about my amber necklace for a long time. Where is it? I have not seen that beautiful amber thing for countless years – indeed, I cannot remember when I last saw it. I would never have sold it, nor given it away. It was my father's, and he had a tragic and violent death in Turkey. How could I have forgotten about such a beautiful and valuable thing? I only know that it is lost forever. How sad! My final thought: Could Madame Prince have magicked it away after all? Ah well, if she did succeed, I forgive her, because she must have been supernaturally clever to do so!

I was always learning from the Gypsies. They seemed to have the kind of knowledge that I wanted and that was not to be found in published books. At least half of my knowledge of herbal medicine has come to me from the Gypsies. I have been able to write two books on veterinary herbs, one of which surprised me by achieving publication in four countries.

I owe much to the Gypsies. They even taught me how to train animals using one's own will power on a dog, horse, bird, or whatever one desired to make obedient to one's commands. I have seen Gypsies calling wild birds to their hands merely by imitative whistling. They taught me how to call to owls. I have trained my Afghan hounds, owls and falcons to be free and return when called. I have seen Gypsies really talking with goats, especially with billy goats who understood everything that was said to them, and then answer back. The Gypsies also possess remarkable powers over wild horses and can make them rideable very speedily. Gypsies' horses are very good to own – although it is known that unless Gypsies like you they are apt to trick you into buying a worthless horse that they would not care to own themselves. My most beautiful horse ever, Willow, was purchased from a family of Yorkshire Gypsies whose only employment was horse-trading the famous "kakkis" of the moorlands; I love them!

With special skills of willpower, physical strength, and understanding of animal and bird mentality (as if the Gypsies had inherited some of the powers of King Solomon), it is understandable that many of the best animal trainers are Gypsies. Despite popular contrary opinion, it is rare that the Gypsies command the obedience of animals by cruelty.

The Hungarian bear tamers seem an exception to that fact, for they tame the wild bears and make them perform their strange dances through memory of pain inflicted. The Hungarian bear leaders are considered very low caste among their fellow Gypsies. They train the bears by burning their feet and backsides on red-hot stones, the burnings inflicted whenever special strains of music are played on drum or pipe. The bears come to learn that if they dance without delay and well enough, they will not get hurt and furthermore will be given sweetmeats that they like in reward. So they dance their slow measures, with their small eyes rolling and afraid.

A modern King of the Gypsies, Iono Yovanovitch, or Vaida Voevod III, King of the Romanies, came to Jerusalem to represent the Gypsies at the Eichmann trial. He says that one of the principal Gypsy tribes is the *Roudari* (which means "friends of animals and wild beasts") and that he belongs to that tribe. I must belong also.

He gives the other principal tribes of Gypsies today as the *Kalderasha* (copper smiths), the *Tshurarea* (craftsmen in gold and silver), and the *Manouch* (general traders). He says that Gypsy history tells, concerning Gypsy skill with metals, that Boaz, when fighting the Moabites, discovered the enemy's secret: that they had Gypsies making their long spears for them. Boaz enticed the Gypsies over to his side and won the battles.

King Vaida Voevod III says one encouraging thing concerning the future of the world: that we are now leaving the Pisease [Piscean] Age, the epoch of the fishes, and moving into the Acquariase [Aquarian] Age, which means Fraternal Brotherhood. He says that Gypsies have always taught their children to ignore the false boundaries of the world, that the world belongs to all men [*sic*] equally, all are brothers [*sic*].

There is Gypsy magic in passionate Romany dancing and singing, in which all Gypsies in all lands excel, with perhaps the exception of the Gypsies of England and Germany, who often perform ungainly step dances. The Gypsy harp music of Wales used to be wonderful, though it is seldom heard nowadays.

Jan Yoors, who knows the Gypsies so well, being of Gypsy descent himself, describes the dancing of the girls and women as having the sensuous beauty of swans and the swiftness of hawks and falcons.

New York friends of mine whom I took along with me to Gypsy *ofisas* were able to enjoy that natural and beautiful dancing. Madame Star's family, in the Bowery *ofisa* on

Houston Street, were very good dancers. Marie (Madame Star) told me that many boys in her family, or her relations' families, earned excellent money in New York and elsewhere combining dancing entertainment with shoe shining. Some of the Gypsy boys, working in Times Square during the Christmas season, were bringing home as much as eight or ten dollars a day (in those days, a significant amount).

On occasion some of my friends surprised the Gypsies. There was Sunny Shay of Long Island, for instance. She performed a thrilling scarf dance for the Star family. Sunny had once been a professional dancer before she took up the raising of Afghan hounds, with which she won world fame. She was still very light on her feet and that night on Houston Street, inspired by the applauding hands of the many Gypsies present, and perhaps especially by a good-looking group of Gypsy men, she danced beautifully! The Gypsies thanked me for bringing her along to give them such pleasure.

Then there was Georges Brunon, the Paris artist whom I introduced to the Gypsies of Granada. He made skillful pencil sketches of our Gypsy friends and gave them to those whom he sketched. Many of his drawings still hang on the walls of Gypsy caves of Sacromonte. In turn, Georges won his first fame through the Gypsies. A big oil painting inspired by the Gypsies of Granada, called simply "*Les Gitanes*," was hung in the famed Paris exhibition of Le Salon d'Automne, where it received much attention.

When I was in New York, troupes of Spanish Gypsy dancers accompanied by guitarists appeared on television and at night clubs and were well liked. Many Hungarian Gypsy violinists found work as entertainers in New York restaurants. The Golden Fiddle on Second Avenue was one place where Hungarian Gypsy music could be heard nightly.

My children and I spent our second New Year's Eve in New York in the company of Gypsy friends gathered in Times Square. There was singing and dancing and kissing and bottles of wine passed around. As a background there was the pushing mob of New York's famed New Year's Eve drunks.

Because my non-Gypsy friends all know that I love the Gypsies, they often tell me of their own experiences with the Gypsies in America. Here are two that I like.

Charles Swenk's parents owned a general food store on the main route for New York City. Bands of Gypsies would call there frequently to stock up on country foods before going on to New York. The Swenk family found that after each visit from the Gypsies, quantities of produce were missing from their shop, especially things from open barrels, such as potatoes, apples, cereal grains, and such things. The parents decided on a plan to control the Gypsy pillaging of their shop. As they had numerous children, seven little Swenks in all, they would station a child at the side of every Gypsy adult who entered, and the child would have to follow the Gypsy around the shop and see that nothing was taken without due payment being made. The plan worked very well. On the arrival of every Gypsy caravan, a brass tray would be beaten and the call, "the Gypsies!" sent out, and the children would take up their positions alongside the invading enemy. The Gypsies were not angered but amused. They laughed outright at the shop's new organization and continued to patronize the Swenk store. They even bought Mrs. Swenk bunches of wildflowers, a thing they had never done before.

The Gypsies are indeed often contemptuous of the non-Gypsy who will allow himself to be tricked by the keener wits of the Romanies. When they themselves are outwitted, they admire those who are capable of this.

Mrs. Isabel Hurd and her son Roger had an apple farm in Tioga County in central New York State. Gypsies often called on them because they were well received by the Hurds, who liked Gypsies. Mrs. Hurd remembers once admiring the magnificent teeth of a Gypsy man visiting them. Pleased, the Gypsy wanted to demonstrate the strength of his teeth, and he stepped up to the door-post and bit a big piece out of the wood. The mark on the door-post showing the Gypsy's bite still remains and is carefully preserved.

A Gypsy woman once told Mrs. Hurd that she knew that she must have lost a baby at an age when it was considered too early to name a baby.

"But," the Gypsy informed her, "your dead baby is so sad at not having a name that he is making you feel miserable." Mrs. Hurd told me that the Gypsy was right. A baby son, her second, and last child, died soon after birth. She had never named it, and spoke of the baby to her first son as "your poor little brother." After the Gypsy's visit, Mrs. Hurd named the baby boy Mark, and had it carved on his gravestone. Ever afterwards, when speaking of him, she called him by name, thanks to the Gypsies' visit.

It was Mrs. Hurd and her son who told me the names of different apples in their orchard, which sounded like poetry: Maiden Blush (pale gold apple with pink tinge), Wolf River, Seek-No-Further (an Indian apple), Rhode Island Greening, Golden Greening, Snow King, Duchess of Oldenburg, Transparent (having almost transparent skin and flesh), Red Astrakhan, Bellflower, Spy, Golden Soul, Copper King, Ruby Red, Honeymoon, Golden Belle, Amber Soul, Redskin.

Who could write of wandering Gypsies and of American apples and not remember that wonderful wanderer, Johnny Appleseed!

John Chapman died a little more than a hundred and fifty years ago. The people of Ohio built a monument to him and Sam Houston, a truly great American, made a speech on the unveiling of the statue. He said: "This old man was one of the most useful citizens of the world, in his humble way. Johnny Appleseed, yours has been a labor of love, and generations yet unborn will rise up and call you blessed."

My children loved to hear about Johnny Appleseed, and my boy read all that he could about him. Who was he? A real person who became a legend. A pioneer American who devoted his life to planting apple trees and accordingly was given the name of "Appleseed." He considered that his mission on earth. He arrived in Ohio wearing a coffee sack, and for a hat, a saucepan. He tramped America barefoot, summer and winter. He brought with him to Ohio a Bible and a sack of seeds from the cider mills of Pennsylvania.

When Ohio became quite settled, Johnny Appleseed sought quieter places in Indiana. There he was friend to both white settlers and Indians, and to animals and birds and even snakes. Johnny Appleseed, in common with many naturalists, possessed great healing powers, and he healed many Indians who in turn taught him their herbal medicine lore. He often warned white settlers of forthcoming Indian attacks. After fights between whites and Indians, he would seek out the wounded on both sides, healing all with herbal medicines, love, and prayer. For many years Johnny Appleseed was followed on his travels through the American countryside by a wolf, which he had saved from a hunter who had killed the cub's mother. He tamed it to an obedience greater than that of any dog.

My children talked about Johnny Appleseed whenever they ate American apples, though I felt sure that Johnny would not approve of the modern poison sprays being used on the apples. They wanted to know if I thought that the apples had come from one of the trees he had planted. Before leaving America they named a doll after the wandering apple-tree planter. They loved him indeed.

Juliette and friends; people of the earth

Chapter Five

Snow White and the Indians

The rough weather of typical New York winters and early springs did not often keep my children and me indoors. I enjoyed walking in Manhattan when the storms were blowing and there was snow underfoot. Also, how could one learn about a city unless one walked its streets and parks and explored the outskirts? I would have liked the snow deeper. Snow, whenever it came, made the streets quite beautiful for awhile, when all was turned from dark gray into scintillating new white, and city lights were reflected there, making stretches look like glittering old medieval samite cloth.

I have seen pictures of old New York when most of the city went around on sleighs. The people sat in horse-driven sleigh-buses and were subjected to the typical New York street sport of snowball pelting, Broadway being one of the favorite sites where the pelters would gather!

New Yorkers still speak about the Great Blizzard of 1888, where two hundred persons in the city were killed by snow. During the blizzard the snow, blown by strong winds, had fallen without cessation for three days and nights and drifted higher than ten feet, in parts.

The deepest snowdrifts that we witnessed during our winters in New York were about three feet, during our second winter. In nearby New Jersey, at Lambertville, the drifts were often deeper, and many days we were snowbound in the James Hewitts' old farmhouse, where we were staying with them. During the deep snow times at Goat Hill Road, the wild deer would come down from the foothills and roam the farmlands.

In New York, my children, in company with the friends they made along Second Avenue and down 78th Street, played the international games of snowmen-making and snowball fighting. I became wearied in time of drying snow-soaked woolen gloves and socks and stockings, and boots filled with melting ice.

Most of our walking around in New York was done in the Manhattan area. That borough, composed of a rocky island, is considered the most important in New York. The population is many millions, composed of all nationalities, and increases during the working hours of every day with the millions more of workers who come in from the suburbs or from the adjoining states of New Jersey, Connecticut, even Pennsylvania. Manhattan has the reputation of harboring the largest number of foreigners of any city in the world. There has been a rocketlike speed of growth in population and buildings since the Dutch first settled on Manhattan Island alongside the few Indian inhabitants in possession there.

The tallest skyscrapers are in Manhattan, and many of the largest schools and colleges, so that the streets are often thronged with students. The most famous theatrical district in the world is also there: an area of fascination.

Most of the early history of New York was enacted on Manhattan Island. One of New York's items of history that I liked was that the first carpet in New York was owned by the pirate Captain Kidd, in his Manhattan home.

The great rivers of the north – the Hudson River – and the east – the East River – surround Manhattan, meeting in

New York harbor and forming the boundaries of the borough, with the Harlem River, of treacherous waters, dividing Manhattan from the Bronx in the north.

The East River was close to our apartment on Second Avenue. We walked down 78th Street and across First Avenue directly to the river. The winter winds sweeping down the river used to pound on the windows at the rear of our apartment on the 78th Street side, rattling the glass and demanding the entry that we usually gave to the winds.

We took almost daily morning walks along the East Riverside. If the factories had not been there in such close proximity, poisoning the air, the East River walks would have been very pleasant. It was enjoyable to see the strange assortment of watercraft, big and small, passing up and down the river. My children and I liked the music of their horns. Sometimes it was sweet and shrill like water birds, other times low and hoarse like the croaking of toads.

The boats passed beneath the great bridges that spanned the river, the various ships and other craft appearing as small as water beetles, contrasting with the immensity of the bridges. Everyone who comes to New York marvels at the bridges; they are beautiful and wonderfully made, and Americans are rightly proud of them. The gray bridges looked to me like the spinal columns of prehistoric mammoths, arched over the waters. The Triborough was our nearest bridge, and its crossing traffic could be seen high in the sky.

Along the riverside we nearly always had the seagulls for company. Sometimes, though rarely, we saw wild fowl passing far overhead, duck skeins mostly. One winter evening of threatening snow, we were surprised to see wild geese passing over New York where the United Nations building stands alongside the river. The great gray birds flew over in typical arrow-tip formation, trailing their dark legs and resting their breasts on the air. We heard distinctly above the city traffic the distant, thrilling honking of the geese, wanderers of the world passing along the sky routes in absolute freedom.

It is said of the American Indians, when they were first confined in reservations, that they gave little trouble until the wild geese were passing overhead; then unbearable nostalgia for their former lives of freedom and for the lonely places would come over them, and for weeks they would be rebellious, unmanageable, and often dangerous.

It is in the East River that the bodies of knifed or bullet-ridden gangsters are said to be seen floating, or the bodies of suicides. We never saw any, only the occasional water-swollen body of an unwanted drowned cat, the eyes pecked out by seagulls.

One evening we had an unpleasant adventure. We were running our Afghan hound along the East River walk when a big, overweight man with a squashed-looking face (he looked like a boxer or wrestler) approached us, bringing with him a snorting boxer dog on a chain. He said he would like to join us in our running. I replied that he and his boxer would frighten our Afghan hound and that we would rather he did not follow us. He insisted that he would run also. So I told my children that we should get away quickly and leave the unpleasant character behind. The entire area was deserted, except for us and that menacing man.

We began to run, and the big man and the snorting dog began to run. Soon it became a chase, and we were disorganized. Instead of our leaving the man behind, it was my children who were outpaced, and I was alone along the East River with the man chasing after me. The river path was entirely deserted; there was traffic on the road, but no one took any notice of the runners. If they saw us, they probably thought we were enjoying ourselves.

When I was getting tired of running, I decided to unleash my Afghan hound, which would enable me to run more easily and to double back past the man on that narrow path. I hoped that the Afghan, being free, would upset the boxer dog. And that was what happened: I slipped past the man and was soon within sight of my children again. I told them to catch the Afghan when she came close to them. We all hurried back to Second Avenue and never again went along the East River after dark! Therefore we missed seeing the wild geese, ducks and other birds that sometimes flew by at dusk, over that river.

We experienced another incident by day that I will never forget, and which I recall whenever I see the big freeways of America with their teeming, crushing vehicles. We had now acquired the habit of giving Cingane, our Afghan hound, her freedom along the East River walk. When we

Fuego, Afghan guardian of travel, with collar of blue Turkish beads (against the evil eye) and a silver charm (hand of Fatima).

wanted to catch her we would block her way across the narrow path and put her on the leash. It was a pleasure to see her racing to and fro along the concrete path; like all the greyhound breed, Afghan hounds glory in their speed.

One mid-morning an iron gate leading from the walk into the expressway, which we had never seen open, had been left open. Cingane disappeared out of sight, and then to our horror we saw her in the expressway seeking swift death from the thronging vehicles. Afghan hounds, unlike most dogs, have no road sense. They like to race down the very center of such places. Many have been killed on roads and railway tracks, including my travel companion of years, the red-golden Afghan Fuego, run down on a New York highway when in the charge of friends. Now our Afghan hound played around the cars that sped along at their usual rapid pace, the drivers never suspecting that they would be meeting with a big dog out there on the fenced-off road. Spectators along the river walk gathered to watch the incredible sight of a dog in the midst of the New York traffic.

Cingane refused to heed our shouted pleas to return to us. At last she found herself really free of the confining fenced-in path, and she was enjoying her liberty. The spectators around us said that the dog would be killed any minute and that it would be better if my children did not watch her any more. A man said that a stray dog had gotten onto a Los Angeles freeway once and caused six cars to pile up on top of each other in a terrible crash, which would have cost the dog's owner a fortune if the dog had not been an ownerless cur.

The brakes of the cars made frightful screaming sounds as drivers braked rapidly to avoid hitting our dog. In the midst of the terror I saw a car slow down, close to Cingane, and the car door opened. A Chinese woman stretched forward, trying to drag the dog into her car to save her. The horrified expression on the woman's face as she tried to help the dog well demonstrated to me the terrible danger. But Cingane slipped away from the would-be saving hands and was back in the midst of the traffic again. Only that attempt to catch her seemed to have frightened her, for a few minutes later she headed towards us, each step that she took nearly being her last one as the cars came upon her. She moved to where we were and showed intelligence by then flattening herself against the railings to avoid being struck by the near cars.

I slipped my hand between the railings and caught hold of our dog's collar, and then put the leash onto the clasp. A tall man who had been among the watchers said he would bend over and lift our dog over the railings to safety, if she would not bite him. I assured the man that he would not be bitten, and in minutes our Afghan was back at our side, miraculously saved. What had saved her from what seemed an inevitable, painful death? Our prayers perhaps, and our love for the dog, but most probably her own beauty. When the car drivers sighted her, they could not bear to hit and thus destroy her. Only equaled by the Arabian Saluki, Afghans are considered the most beautiful dogs in all the world. They are of the greyhound type, but clad in flowing, silken hair of the softness and fineness of mohair. They walk over the ground as if they had springs in their feet; they go by with such a prancing gait. And they have gazelle eyes, beautiful, almond-shaped, lambent, far-seeing eyes. The Queen of Sheba brought with her a brace of Afghan hounds among her gifts to King Solomon, it is told.

All our friends who heard of the dog's escape from the East River/FDR Drive traffic agreed that it was a miracle. Cingane was never again allowed off the leash anywhere in New York except in a few areas of Central Park, far away from any passing traffic.

Central Park was also in easy walking distance of our apartment, going in the opposite direction from the East

River, away from the front part of the house. This area of parkland, 840 acres in extent, defies the inroads of the building projects pressing in on all sides. It is called the most valuable piece of greenery on earth. In the park are miles of winding footpaths and bridle paths, some of them pleasantly rural. And there are quite extensive stretches of water also, where wild and tame waterfowl can be seen and boating and skating are enjoyed in season.

Central Park is the best-known of all the over one hundred big and little parks of Greater New York. It stretches from 59th Street to 110th Street. But even there, in all that stretching acreage of land, "Curb Your Dog" was the rule, as it was in every park in New York City. Every open place had its restrictive notice: "No dogs, bicycles, peddlers allowed." Nowhere to let a dog run in the freedom essential to health and the proper digestion of food, which is much dependent on proper oxygenation of the bloodstream through active and sufficient exercise. Dogs cannot be kept in health without exercise.

Dogs are becoming highly important in New York life to safeguard their owners' property against the hordes of thieves that molest that city. If I had had our dog with me when the window cleaner came to our apartment, he would not have been able to steal anything. We had been told later by our friend Florine Molinari of Greenwich Village that the same window cleaner had been in the Village. He had come to their apartment with the same story of being sent by the owner of the house, and he had cleaned their windows, but had not been able to steal from her because their cocker spaniel, bristling with rage at the end of a leash on which they had had to put her because of her dislike of the man, had followed the cleaner from room to room, snarling and agitated the whole time, until he departed.

I have exercised my Afghan hounds in the parks of many cities. Hyde Park and Kensington Gardens in London, where I once used to exercise eight adult Afghans in a pack, and in Paris's Bois de Boulogne, and Madrid's Prada, and never was I threatened with paying fines – of as much as twenty dollars in some places in New York – if I unleashed my dog.

In Central Park there is a monument erected to Balto, a husky dog. To the memory of Balto's faithful courage and magnificent strength used in the service of man. He was the leader of the sled team that won the great moose race in the time of the explorer Amundsen, and which team Amundsen took north with him before his discovery of the Pole, and which further brought him safely through many dangerous blizzards. But if Balto himself had been in this modern Central Park, he would have had to be confined on a leash, his limbs not properly exercised, his health declining. A dog statue in that park seemed a mockery to me!

Friends in New York who love their dogs, and worry about them never being able to run on the earth in freedom, take their dogs to Central Park and other of the large parks in the very early hours of the morning, to let them exercise well for a short while. They make themselves look as poor as possible, wearing wool Babushka scarves swathed around their faces. In that way, if caught by park police with their dogs off the leash, they hope to escape with the lower fine of two dollars or so, which they think well worth paying weekly to safeguard their dogs' health.

I wish that in every city of the world the people would set aside a tract of land in one or two of the parks where dog owners could let their dogs run off the leash. The land could be fenced in if necessary. Only the area should be changed every six months, liming the old piece of land in the meanwhile to prevent canine worm infection, which is common from public parks where many city dogs, unhealthy from an unnatural diet of canned and processed foods, are exercised.

In some parts of Central Park I unleashed our Afghan hound. I was never caught and fined. If I had been caught, I would have pretended not to understand the American language. That was another method that my New York friends used. For the rest, I ran the dog on her leash.

It seems that New York men are unused to seeing women run, since they used to hiss after me amorously: their "s-s-s" sounded like serpents in Central Park. The attraction might however have been the colored stockings

Central park snow: Rafik and Luz with their Afghan hound

that I wore! Only I was not alone in wearing colored stockings: they were popular then among New York's women and little girls. I had first seen such stockings worn by many American women on the ship coming over, and I had thought how strange they looked after the drab black or fawn hose of the Spanish women to which I had grown accustomed. The New York shops were selling stockings in all colors – red, blue, purple, pink, orange, green. I favored green! My little daughter liked to wear yellow! These stockings were very warm and hard-wearing.

I wish I could have gone barefoot winter and summer, like Johnny Appleseed! Barefoot Gypsy style may have been possible in the snow and over ice when it lay on natural ground, but the cold striking up from sidewalks of concrete froze one to the marrow of one's bones. Cleaning snow slush from shoes and stockings gave endless work. During our second winter in New York the city was using salt for snow clearance. An annual purchase of salt to cleanse New York City of snow was said to cost around two million dollars for the winter of 1960–61. I think that the salt made more mess than the snow. Everything was splashed white: footwear, skirt and trouser hems, the telephone boxes, and the vehicles. Taxi drivers were angry about their soiled taxis.

Our hound chased the gray squirrels across Central Park, chased them among the piled leaves that had turned varying shades of yellows, reds, and browns because frost had touched them. In some places in the park, fires were being kindled on the pyramids of the piled winter leaves, and the scent of woodsmoke drifted pleasantly around us and made me think of Gypsies and American Indians.

My children always hastened to the giant statues – of Alice in Wonderland and the characters from that wonderful tale all gathered around her and of Hans Christian Andersen, creator of beloved and undying fairy tales – that were a feature of Central Park. Never before had we seen children clambering over statues. In Central Park, the boys and girls swarmed over Alice and Hans; and my two, at first shyly and then boldly, clambered upon the statues in the company of the other children.

Adults standing by told me that the children's boots kept the statues well polished, and therefore they never turned green in New York's damp-weather spells as did others of the city's statues on which the children had no climbing rights. We saw a colored boy spitting on the face of Hans Andersen, making streams of spittle. He told his mother that he was making tears for "Mister Hans's ol' face." The spittle ran in a shining stream down the broad forehead and around the big nose. It was nicer to see rain washing down over the great face, or the snow plastered there and then melting.

We were told that in the summertime readings from Alice in Wonderland and from the Andersen fairy tales were given by professional actors and actresses for the New York children gathered by the statues for that purpose.

There were many pleasures for children in Central Park. There was a merry-go-round, also pony- and horse-driven carriages in which visitors to the park could make a pleasant tour of its spreading acres. There was a big pond for the sailing of toy boats, and there was also winter skating on the several wide stretches of water enclosed in the area.

All the children enjoyed feeding and petting the park birds and squirrels, many of which were quite tame.

It is important for children in towns to see and know animals. I was told that a milking cow in a van was taken around to the most urban of the New York schools so that children should see the animal that gave them that blue-white, pasteurized, lifeless substance obtained from cartons and bottles called milk.

Before we left New York we took bunches of spring flowers to the children's statues in Central Park, for the pleasure that they had given us. Rafik also wanted to take a bunch of flowers to the grave of Peter Stuyvesant, New York's first governor. Rafik had been reading a book about Stuyvesant and old New York, and he much wanted to see the church of St. Mark's in the Bowery, where the governor's bones were entombed.

This time we purchased daffodils. Rafik had wanted tulips as soon as he had seen them in the flower shop, telling me that tulips were the national flower of Stuyvesant's birth land, Holland, and his favorite flower. But the tulips in New York cost a dollar each and were made up into arranged bunches of one dozen blooms. I persuaded the flower seller to let us have one tulip from a bunch of yellow beauties, thus matching our daffodils.

The lady of the shop was interesting. She was from Romania, and she was bemoaning to me the fact that there

was no one to pierce ears properly in North America. She showed me her teenaged daughter who had had her ears pierced twice by a New York doctor at five dollars a time, and each time the ear-holes had turned septic and had to be allowed to close up again. She had noticed the great holes in my ears, big enough to pass a meat skewer through. Berber Arabs on the island of Djerba in Tunisia had made those holes for me so that I could wear their earrings, enlarging on the original smaller work of an English Gypsy using a darning needle, and then ash off her cigarette as an antiseptic.

I advised her to take her daughter the third time to a nearby Gypsy family. The flower lady told me that she had a fine pair of family earrings waiting for her daughter's wearing. She then very unexpectedly added another yellow tulip to our bunch of flowers, as a gift for my "kind information." She said further that while I and my children had been standing at her shop window admiring her flowers, she had been admiring my big Bedouin silver earrings with the green stones and hoping that we would enter her shop!

When we arrived with our flowers at St. Mark's, we found the church locked, and we could not enter. But having come so far we were determined to leave our gift. Therefore we searched around until we found a man who knew something of the church, and he showed us from outside the wall the position where Stuyvesant was buried. We tossed the flowers over in that direction. The weather was all ice. It would keep the flowers fresh until the church was opened, and then, I hoped, the caretaker would put the flowers in their proper place. I had borrowed pencil and paper from the man and written out Stuyvesant's name, and Rafik had added a message that he was pleased to know "that Stuyvesant had been nice to the American Indians," and therefore he loved him.

The American Indians! As a fellow herbalist and naturalist, I had them almost daily in my thoughts throughout my time in North America. I met with some Americans of pure Indian blood, and I met also with Americans who had known Native Americans well. I had learned much from American Indian medicine, and I admired Indian arts as shown in their handicrafts, especially their wonderful jewelry, which friends of mine owned, and which was also sometimes seen in the New York shops.

Apart from the Museum of the American Indian and many Indian exhibits in the great Museum of Natural History on Central Park West, there was also the Indian crafts shop – The Tepee – where all manner of traditional objects could be purchased, from feathered war bonnets and decorative wooden peace pipes to embroidered leather moccasins, silverware, and pottery.

The first trading in Manhattan between the Dutch newcomers and the native Americans, was in skins. A shipment of 7,246 beaver skins and 675 skins of otter – obtained from "the wild men" in exchange for cheap trinkets, mirrors, and cloth of low quality – were shipped from New York (then New Amsterdam) to Holland.

The trading was unfair, as it has been throughout history when civilized men trade with "the natives" and then enslave them and deprive them of their land and their rights.

Now the wild Americans are gone, or are mostly gone. Now and then I met with a person who said that he or she was of pure Indian blood. Usually the truth of their claim was shown by the beautiful eyes of almond shape and the high cheekbones, also the upright carriage.

Paul Matthews was one Indian whom I admired, of Cherokee blood. He composed music. I hope that the music of the American Indian, music for the flute and the drum, will never be lost. On simple, hand-carved flutes the braves would play their love music to the maidens.

My children, in Mexico, found two very old Indian whistles made of clay. Deep burial in cliff sides had preserved them. One was shaped like a primitive water jar, only music, not water, dripped from its many skillfully made holes. The other was shaped like a bird-woman, with the head and form of a bird but the breasts of a woman. That clay thing makes the sweetest, far-carrying whistle music I have ever heard. It sounded like waterside birds such as the curlews.

Then there was Paul Greene, who worked in a medical laboratory in New York, of pure Cherokee descent on his mother's side. He possessed the black skin and characteristic hair of the Negro, inherited from his father who was half-Negro, half-Irish. Paul had the carriage and walk of the typical American Indian, and he told me that from his Indian mother he had inherited inordinate pride, which caused him much suffering on account of his black skin. When I invited him to have an Indian meal with us of succotash (corn and beans) and sweet peppers and wild rice and fruits and nuts, I noticed disapproving glances from other residents in the building as the dark-skinned man ascended the stairs in the company of me and my children. It was the same when I brought Gypsies home with me. I was used to the hostility of one race towards another; I was used to it, but I regretted it and would never accept it. Fortunately, in later years it has become much less.

I expect that the Gypsies would be happier on their former unpopulated hillsides, and in the lonely forests and plains.

In America I also came to know Teddy Drinkerd, a Seminole Indian from Florida. Her husband, likewise a Seminole, told me that his people were unique among the American Indians in not signing any treaties with the whites. To this day they possess lands, power, and absolute freedom in America. Their swamp territory protected them from white conquest; they had known the secret ways through the swamps and had been able to fight with better success there.

Teddy Drinkerd is a professional dancer; she is sometimes partnered by her husband, who has the physique of a good dancer. When I first met Teddy I thought she was a Spanish or Mexican Gypsy. I asked her about this, using an indirect approach. Teddy told me that she was American Indian, but that I was not the first person to associate her with the Gypsies, and that her Gypsy resemblance had once earned her fifty dollars in less than fifteen minutes. She told me that she had once been dancing her American Indian dances in a mixed group taken to a very important Hollywood club where many famous people were gathered. A non-Gypsy woman was performing Gypsy dances. The producer came to her to say that the Gypsy dancing had been so disappointing to the audience that now seeing Teddy he felt sure she could "dance Gypsy" far better than the woman who had just performed. He offered her fifty dollars to lend her Gypsy costume to Teddy for a few minutes, and he would pay Teddy a further fifty dollars above her arranged fee if she would put on the costume and dance just as the mood took her.

Teddy told me that as she put on the costume, which was a genuine one, old and beautiful, the spirit of the Gypsies completely possessed her, and she knew that she had never danced better in her life.

In an old document in the Gypsy section of the library of the small Provence town of Les Saintes de la Mer, the Gypsies are associated with the American Indians. The document says that legend tells that the Indian people came from the part of the hemisphere where the sun rises, and the Gypsies come from a part beyond where the sun sets. Perhaps the Indians felt this, for the rising sun was the motif on many of their tents.

Teddy told me about some of her American Indian dances and the costumes that she wore for them. There was the Dance of the Green Corn and the Dance of the Yellow Corn; the Dance of the Sun; the Fire Dance; the Dance of the Buffalo Hunts; and the Bear Dance (slow and solemn).

An Indian herbalist told me that before many of their dances the braves would rub their bodies with bunches of wild herbs: the fragrant prairie sage for dances of war and marriage, wild garlic for dances to ward off plagues from their encampments, and for their most famous dance of all, the tragic Ghost Dance, the bitter herb wormwood.

The American Indian Ghost Dance was created out of despair. The Indians began to dance their Ghost Dance when they knew that they were doomed: the ruthless civilization of the white men, together with their greed for Indian land, would lead to their near annihilation.

The killing of the Indians began with the Spanish conquest of large parts of the Americas. Cruel ways and an overwhelming lust for gold characterized most of the Spanish conquerors. The Spanish often intermarried with the natives, and therefore often loved them, as is shown in Mexico.

When they landed, the Pilgrim Fathers, some claim, fell first upon their knees in humble prayer, and then fell upon the natives, destroying them. But the founding fathers paid close attention to their native neighbors and used many of their ideas in creating the United States government.

Perhaps no other people have so much stirred the interest and imagination of the civilized world as have the North American Indians. Countless Americans today deplore the means – broken spoken promises and broken written agreements – by which the white race gained possession of so much Indian land. It is strange, like a sign from God, that such a large percentage of land considered worthless when given to the Native Americans has since been found to be rich in oil, uranium, and other valuable commodities!

Snow White and the Indians

Native American Indians say that in every place where they were mistreated, that cruel plant – poison ivy – now flourishes. Certainly there is an abundance of it, and its sister poison oak, growing over much of North America. This plant of the sumac family is a perennial of most persistent and spreading growth; it is the terror of American gardens and countryside. It looks like an innocent, three-leafed form of Virginia creeper. But it contains an oil – present at all times of the year – that is a baneful poison. The swelling and irritation that its touch produces on the human skin defeats words to properly tell about it, and likewise, at least for days, it defeats all known remedies.

While in America, I experienced poison ivy skin poisoning several times, and I found the old Gypsy remedy of pulped dock (*Rumex crispus*) leaves, useful against all forms of skin irritation, to be by far the most effective treatment. I cured myself and others with that simple remedy. When dock leaves are not available, slightly diluted lemon juice is helpful. Also jewelweed (*Impatiens pallida*) is helpful.

[I rub fresh jewelweed on poison ivy rash for fast relief. But, for the best results, I boil fresh jewelweed, including the reddish roots, in cold water until the liquid turns orange. Then, I drink the liquid freely. It acts more quickly than cortisone to reduce swelling and itching. I keep a quart of this jewelweed broth frozen, just in case I need it in the winter.]

Poison ivy is difficult to eradicate from any land where it has established itself. Burning spreads the poison by smoke, and all who are within reach of the smoke become as badly poisoned as if they had touched the ivy itself.

Then, as further punishment, the Indians taught their white conquerors to smoke tobacco, while the Indians themselves smoked harmless herbs and grasses. Tobacco is called Indian Poison Weed in old books. And Indian poison weed enslaves men. It is highly addictive. Thus the punishment is still effective after all this time.

The needs of the American Indians were small and simple. They often lived like wandering Gypsies, keeping only such possessions as fitted a nomad way of life, things that they could carry with them.

From feathers and beads, tree barks and grasses, leather, woolen strands and beads, they made the most useful and beautiful things. They adorned their horses and not merely themselves. They made streaming feathered bonnets for their horses, which they near worshipped. Their fearless horse-riding gave them the speed of the winds and helped them war against the white men. American Indians are recognized as some of the most skilled and daring horsemen of the world, and the Gypsies should also be remembered in this respect.

One thing for which the American Indians were much hated and punished, was the crime of scalping. And yet it was the English themselves who taught the natives to scalp their victims! Baynes Barron of Hollywood, who often acted in Western films and knew much about the Indians, first told me about this. (And I later read about it in an authoritative book.)

The English, when they killed American Indians, used to cut off and ship back to England, as curios, the scalps of the "wild men" with their strange and beautiful long black hair. American Indians who witnessed the scalpings passed the news to the other tribes; soon scalping was a vengeance rite against the whites. Old Western-life prints show white men crowding into barbershops to have their heads shaved bald as a precaution against scalping when they had to be in Indian-dominated territory.

The English once took some Indian "savages" in full red war paint (thus the name "redskins") to Queen Victoria's court, where the dignified bearing of the Indians greatly impressed the queen and put to shame those who had gathered to stare and laugh at the strangers.

Once an American artist friend, Emily Norfeld, put an old Indian blanket over my shoulders. It had been the property, a century ago, of a Navajo chief, and the chief had given it to her brother, also an artist and another staunch friend of the American Indians. The beautiful weave, pattern, and coloring of the blanket cloak, and the smell of horses still upon it, so inspired me that I wanted to begin writing about those Indians at once.

Then Emily showed me a very old Navajo silver squaw necklace called "squash blossom," the flowers modeled in silver. Never have I seen a more admirable necklace. The old silver goblet-like flowers of the squash plant hung between the crowding silver leaves. In the center of the necklace hung an amulet with a big green stone in a silver setting, the stone the color of a leaf when it first opens to the light.

The Navajo Indians also gave their name to a beautiful gemstone sold in America. It is a type of pale obsidian, and the jewels are called Navajo Tears, being often in the pearl-drop shape of a human tear. The stones are supposed to be the petrified tears of many Navajo women, shed when lamenting the loss of their men who plunged to their deaths over a mountainside rather than be taken by the American troops who had surrounded them.

Seldom have a people left such a memorable mark on the history of the human race, or made such a lasting impression on the minds of men, as the Indians of America, the first people of New York. Yet, even to this day the Native Americans are losing their land. An esteemed American lawyer, Sol Rosenblatt, told me that in a far part of New York State, a piece of land given to the Indians is now wanted for a power-station project. The Indians do not want to sell their land, for there is still good hunting there, which they have carefully preserved. However, as Mr. Rosenblatt told me bitterly, for like all just men he deplores the treatment meted out to the American Indians, the Indians have lost most legal battles fought.

An artist who knew the American Indians well, and helped them during the Indian war days, was George Catlin. He immortalized – in many sketches – the last days of the American Indian's greatness in America. Catlin pleaded, as late as 1841, for a vast national park to be made across America, to save the Indians and the great buffalo herds. But all that the Indians got were small reserves of land considered unfit for white men to farm where they are subjected to restrictive laws that take all the joy out of the type of life that the natural person likes to live. This shameful genocide must be put right if America wants to be respected by the peoples of the world.

When the natives of the Great Plains saw what was facing them, when they witnessed the greedy destruction of their beautiful trees, whose loss brought drought to their lands, and the mass slayings of the buffalo herds in vengeance and sport, not out of any genuine need for meat, there spread among them the immortal Ghost Dance, to lead them to a heaven where there would be no more white tormentors.

To an Indian brave, Wovoka, the spirit of the Ghost Dance came; it came when he was in a trance state. The dance came at a time when Indian despair was greatest, when famine and disease spread far and wide. It whirled at the speed of wind-blown tumbleweeds through the tribes.

The dance became a new test of physical strength to braves. It replaced the Sun Dance, which had also tested physical strength. The Ghost Dance was often performed to the eerie wailing of the watching women and the howling of the camp dogs.

Now I suppose that much of that agony has gone from the American scene. At least in the city of New York, the only "Indians" in feathered war bonnets, carrying tomahawks and peace pipes that one sees nowadays are little boys playing that everlasting game of cowboys and Indians, out in the streets of monotonous gray concrete instead of on the wild American plains and hills, or by the riversides and lakes.

The Gypsies have been fined and harassed in America in the same way as the Native American Indians, but they have cleverly made no treaties with people of another non-nomadic race as did the Indians; they have never agreed to settle, or cease their comings and goings. The American Gypsies have mostly managed to remain prosperous and happy.

Many people agree that the nomadic races the world over should be allowed, indeed helped, to remain nomadic. They bring to the settled races new talents worth preserving. They bring wonderful stories, songs, music, and other arts, all taken from Nature, with whom they have remained in close contact. They are irreplaceable personalities with unique contributions to make.

Who would dare to try and interfere with the migratory habits of those nomadic birds, the swallows and swifts, and the wild geese and swans, for instance?

This parallel is not farfetched. Think of the "comings and goings" of the Gypsies, and of the Irish and Scottish tinkers also. Godspeed to them! They are beautiful in themselves and in their lives.

I am cheered and encouraged just now by a letter from Irene Soper (author of *The Romany Way*, Ex Libris Press, England, 1995), of England's New Forest. Irene and her husband took over my thatched cottage in a lonely part of this forest. She also inherited my Gypsy friends, who made that cottage a frequent calling place. The Gypsies of Great Britain are yet very defiantly traveling the roads with their horse-drawn wagons (*vardos* or caravans), accompanied by their Gypsy lurcher dogs (a greyhound type).

Gypsy troubadour; Provence

Chapter Six

Leaving No Stone Unturned

Most cities have a sordid side, and New York is no exception. The great cities have to maintain a huge police force and also have to use special vice squads. But, disregarding the human element for the time being, it is a sad thing that part of the sordidness is the ever-present vermin.

When one looks through the pages of New York's telephone books and sees the pages given to Pest Control advertisements, it is surprising to find so much vermin still alive in the city. For me, the hordes of insects and rodents in New York once more prove the failure of chemicals, certainly as compared to the benefits of cleanliness and the use of many herbs that – as has been known for centuries – are effective insect and rodent repellents. In old New York, "osage oranges," which are the fruits of the beautiful red osage, were used as a cockroach exterminator, but now such simple remedies are neglected.

In Harlem there is a rat problem. It has been written about in the newspapers. But the greatest problem, to me, seemed to be the cockroaches. Cockroaches are merely "roaches" in New York. Most New York hardware shops carry advertisements for roach-exterminating powders and pastes.

My children and I met with those beastly brown insects everywhere. We had them in abundance in our apartment.

Most of my friends seemed to have them, even if they lived at a good address on Park Avenue or Madison Avenue. I began to greet every new visitor with the question, "Do you have cockroaches in your apartment?" Thus the greeting was rather like something out of Alice in Wonderland! But the subject was of great interest to me. Most of the replies were in the affirmative. We saw roaches on the walls of a famed Fifth Avenue restaurant. We saw them in good-class pizza shops. (Pizza pie is a very popular food in New York, taken over from Italy.) We stopped buying pizza because we never could be sure whether there had or had not been contamination by roaches.

I suppose most people did not give the matter any thought at all. One only had to see people in the shops buying from uncovered trays or barrels of food, on which dust and grime must settle, and which probably swarmed by night with roaches, ants, and possibly mice, to realize this. I have a firm conviction that the contamination of food by the feet and excretions of vermin is a contributing cause of disease. I took the utmost care to ensure that my children only got clean food.

In my apartment I killed hundreds of roaches before I got them under control: first by starving them away – that is, by not letting them have access to one particle of food on my territory – and then, by sprinkling along their entry places and most favorite paths, a mixture of pungent and bitter herbs [rue, wormwood, tansy] which they could not bear to get on their feet or bodies. Further, I sprinkled around the base of the steam pipes, down which the roaches would descend at night, a thick layer of dried lemon and grapefruit peel.

After every lemon or grapefruit that we ate – and we ate plenty as protection against winter infections – I spread the peel on the steam radiators. When the radiators were turned on, they quickly dried the peels to a brittleness that crushed into tiny fragments at a touch. This crushed peel was sharp to the touch and strong smelling – no vermin liked to tread over it. Within one month I was almost free of the pests which could even be found on the beds and in the bath. Within two months there was never a roach to be seen, and the ants that had also been present in lesser numbers were likewise gone. When I returned one year later to the same apartment for a few days' visit before leaving America, the new occupant, my friend Hermine Haller, told me that the roaches had never returned after my severe treatment of them. I did find the place quite free but noticed a few ants back again – but then, no treatment had been given at all since mine had ended!

As a vegetarian I hate to kill anything. It is told of Buddha, the great vegetarian, that during the rainy season he walked very little because it was a sadness for him to have to crush underfoot the teeming insect life awakened by the rains; and he was one of the greatest walkers, in Tibet and beyond.

But I also believe with Zoroaster, who was also a vegetarian, that the animal kingdom (which includes birds and insects) can be divided into two: the subjects of the good god, Ahura Mazda (Zarathustra), and the subjects of the bad god, Ahriman. The subjects of Ahriman are mostly vermin – noxious insects and rodents and parasitic worms – which bring disease and death to man and therefore may be killed. One test to distinguish these subjects of Ahriman is that they cause man to shudder or to scream involuntarily – even a jumping flea can cause a big man to cry out!

When the cockroaches first came to New York in large numbers they were called Croton bugs, after the big new Croton River dam, built in the early part of the century, which brought the river water to New York. The people believed that the roaches came out of the water. They did not trace their increase to the large new food stores multiplying throughout New York and left out overnight, allowing all kinds of vermin to feed: sacks of flour, pulses, rice, and sugar, cheeses and cooked meats, trays of delicatessen foods, and in the bakeries, stacks of unsold breads, rolls, and buns.

In the old days of New York, Fleischmann's famous bread bakery and restaurant, on the corner of Broadway and 10th Street, used to give away to the poor, every night, all bread that had not been sold from the previous night's baking. The bread queues outside Fleischmann's used to be one of the sights of New York. If all bakeries had worked on that plan, or at least stored away all unsold produce in tied-up sacks, there would be fewer vermin in New York and other cities today.

The Wakay Rock of the American Indians was also a good idea. Every dusk, by strict rule, all food leavings from the camp were taken to a high rock a distance away and left as an offering to the Good Spirits, or to the birds, squirrels, and other creatures of the wild who would accept man's food.

I think one cause of the great vermin problem in New York is that the people, misled by the propaganda of skillful advertising, or on account of their own personal laziness, have relied on the use of chemicals to combat vermin instead of paying attention to absolute cleanliness in the home.

Into the half-cleaned sinks of the average household roaches come to feed on the grease and dirt; they also swarm in company with houseflies to fatten on the steamy fumes from cooking pans, especially meats, and to seek the crumbs dropped around table and chairs. Wooden beds left standing for years, the cracks and wood pores gradually filling with dead skin cells and other excretions from the nightly occupants, likewise mattresses never put out in the cleansing air and sun, dirt-filled floor cracks, all are tempting pastures for the vermin hordes.

Air-conditioning is a great friend of vermin, for the cleansing outdoor air, and especially the cold, vermin-killing air of winter, is never allowed entry. But, as one New York friend said to me, when she cleans the air-conditioning filters at her New York windows, she is thankful to see the black and oily grime that has been excluded from her apartment.

Many New York friends have told me that roaches are harmless as they do not sting or bite. They say that they have had roaches about them all their lives in New York, from childhood to adulthood, and would be lacking something if they did not have them scurrying around their apartments cleaning up the crumbs.

"But they have a horrible smell about them," I said.

They defended the creatures by telling me stories about New York roaches, to prove that those insects have endearing qualities of character. I began to feel mean each time I squashed a roach. Only then I began remembering the disgusting ways of cockroaches: How they swarmed in filthy places and then trod on one's food with the same soiled feet, how they got among one's clean clothes – the yellow type of cockroach in Mexico would even chew holes in clothing – and how they appeared unexpectedly and fell into one's bath water when one was relaxing in it. Here is an account of a cockroach rescue as witnessed by my friend Dana Miller and quoted in defense of the roach family!

A roach was drowning in a glass of milk in a New York apartment. Another roach hastened to its rescue. The rescuer carefully lowered its own body into the milk, meanwhile gripping the rim of the glass firmly with its front feet. The drowning roach then clambered onto the back of its friend, who carried the rescued one carefully back to the dry safety of the kitchen tabletop.

That cockroaches can be intelligent and amusing was told me by another friend, Mildred Fischer, who also told me that she has plenty of roaches in her apartment and does not mind them at all! She believes that a Japanese traveler first brought a cockroach to America as a present to a friend, as he thought the insect was a thing of great beauty. This may be more fiction than fact, but they must have come in from somewhere at some time, and then spread rapidly because of the easy living conditions prevailing. I am sure that there are many more roaches than New Yorkers in that city today.

Mildred told me that a big roach was sitting in a bowl of rice, enjoying the heaped feast there and keeping off all the smaller roaches as it fed at its leisure. The little roaches were seen to gather together and discuss a mass attack. Ten of the smaller roaches bunched together and rushed at the big roach, who was soon dislodged from his position, and the little roaches then settled down to a rice feast themselves, one in turn keeping watch all the time to ensure that the big fellow did not come back until the group had eaten all that they desired.

Another friend, Betty Scott, told me that she had been given a box of chocolates as a Christmas present in which there was a little wooden pig. The pig seemed wonderfully made, for it had most lifelike movements, twitching its tail and ears and winking its eyes, all without stopping. It needed no winding. The friend who gave her the chocolates was tempted to open up the pig to see how it worked. He did, and a live cockroach – which had been the mechanism of the pig – dashed out and made for the chocolates. The smell of the chocolates had made the insect frantic, thus causing the movement of the pig's lightly pinned-on ears and tail, and causing the eyes to seem to wink!

When the famous old Provincetown Theatre – and its restaurant – in Greenwich Village was fumigated, three bucket loads of cockroaches, bedbugs and mice were afterwards collected from the premises.

The presence of bedbugs in New York is shown by the many prominent advertisements in hardware shops promising their extermination. [In 2005, a famous resort in the Catskill Mountains of New York State was sued by a patron who got 500 bedbugs bites in one night.] Mention of bedbugs in the city always recalled to me one of America's famous cartoons by the popular cartoonist Art Young. It shows two slum children peering up at the Manhattan night sky, to be seen only with difficulty on account of the New York skyscrapers towering above them. The slum boy is exclaiming rapturously, "Gee, Annie, look at the stars, thick as bedbugs."

I have not yet finished with New York cockroaches! An American classic by Don Marquis, *Archie and Mehitabel*, is about that familiar resident, a roach named Archie, and his friend, Mehitabel the cat. It is written throughout without capital letters, the explanation being given that the roach who writes the story has not sufficient strength to press down the shift key to get capital letters. Archie begins his story in words unsurprising to all who know the New York cockroaches:

> thank you for the apple peelings in the wastepaper basket
> but your paste is getting so stale i can't eat it . . .
> i have just been reading
> an advertisement of a certain
> roach exterminator.
> the human race little knows
> all the sadness it causes the insect world.

There are many rats and mice in New York, ever increasingly serious. In fact, as time goes by, the rat menace becomes worse. By law all refuse bin lids have to be fitted on those refuse bins out in the street near every apartment house. But as almost all the bins were habitually filled to overflowing, fitting the lids was impossible, and big rats feeding in the bins would often bound down when I passed by late at night before the midnight refuse trucks had been there. My children and I also saw rats running around in a type of circle dance, whenever the moon was full, down in the yard beneath the rear window of our apartment. I believed that if the Pied Piper of Hamelin had stepped through the streets of New York in these modern times of chemical rat poisons, he would still have had an abundant and merry company of rodents following after him!

Old legend says that the Pied Piper of Hamelin was a Gypsy, and that explains his intense anger at the breaking of a spoken promise make to him by the Hamelin mayor and supported by the other city authorities. The Gypsies scorn the way that the non-Gypsy often will lightly break a spoken promise given and further scorn the way that non-Gypsy promises involving money are not considered safe until they are signed and sealed by lawyers.

Gypsies have the reputation for being tricksters; that may be. Since early times they have suffered from the scorn

The author with New Forest Gypsies, Godshill Moors, England

and mistrust and unfair discrimination against them of the non-Gypsy. Among themselves, the spoken word is absolutely binding; they are a people who keep spoken promises.

All the important Gypsy horse and mule dealing that I have witnessed has been done that way: a spoken word and a touching of hands, palm down upon outstretched palm. The deal is binding. No true Gypsy would consider defaulting. In England, I bought my horse from the Gypsies that way. I paid them later. She was a riding mare of great beauty.

In medieval days in Europe, Gypsies were often rat charmers, just as in the East many Gypsies were snake charmers. To charm the rats and mice away from villages and towns to other places where they could be exterminated, the Gypsies played the sweetest and most thrilling music on long pipes made from cat vertebrae, those cat pipes yielding the most dulcet and alluring notes – so old documents relate. In snake charming, the Gypsies played on pipes made instead of the forelegs of cats, to call the snakes to them.

So, the Gypsies tell, the Pied Piper of Hamelin, in his patched two-colored, wide cloak, and his faded, two-colored, tall hat with the tossing long plume, carrying the sweet-voiced pipe of cat vertebrae in his thin dark hands, was a strolling Gypsy who knew well the art of magic and was thus able to lure away with ease, through the music of his flute, the thousandfold rats and mice, and then all the children of Hamelin.

Two clues to his Gypsy identity are in an old Belgian manuscript concerning the legend of Hamelin. One is in the description of the piper's shoes: "the same as worn by the Gypsy men." The second: his clothes of many colors. Patchwork was in former times chosen wear of the Gypsy men. And patchwork is pied, so he was called the Pied Piper.

I cannot tolerate rats. It is well known that the rat population of the world is enormous. If only man would content himself with fighting the vermin population of the world instead of his fellow-men, there would be a sufficiency of food for all, eaten in an atmosphere of lasting peace. If man speeds through space to new planets and is able to settle there, will he take the dirt of the world along with him including the rats and mice? Will he change? Will he bring terror to the good animal population that might be there? Will he prey on the animals, experiment with them, deny them their rights to live their full lifespan as God – or Nature – intended for them?

It is said, that of all creatures, man is the dirtiest, the greatest creator of his own dirt, and of dirt in his dwelling place, often in the company of rats, cockroaches, ants, and silverfish. Even a hog is a seeker of sunshine, whereas the man of the big cities – and it is from there that the people of the world are ruled – shuts himself away from the sun and is content with the light of electricity and the heat of steam pipes, which hiss like serpents in his dirt-gilded apartments.

The first attempt to keep New York clean was in 1702, when house owners had to sweep up all their refuse, and any street dirt around them, into heaps, ready for removal every Saturday. From the Dutch days up to as late as 1825, there was no other garbage collection provided in New York, except for that once-weekly sweeping up. All household refuse was merely flung into the streets, and there hogs were permitted to roam in large numbers, to eat up the garbage. Indeed, passers-by went in danger of being pelted with rotten foodstuffs by persons flinging out garbage from upper windows in New York dwellings. Numerous rats helped the swine in their refuse-eating task. The stench of old New York was a source of astonishment and disgust to visitors from other cleaner American cities, such as Washington, Boston, and Philadelphia, as well as to newcomers to the city (although Boston's rats are also notorious).

Nowadays it is a fineable offense to throw any refuse into the New York streets from any window, although it must be difficult to trace the thrower of an odd rotten apple from the thousandfold windows of a big skyscraper apartment house!

Referring again to rats, there was some excitement and alarm in New York in recent years when a woman on foot was passing over a piece of wasteland and was attacked by a crowd of rats, which ran at her legs, biting at her. Her screams of terror brought people to their doors to witness that remarkable event. A van drove up and pulled the woman into it, saving her from the attacking rats. She must have been quite badly bitten, but nothing more was heard from her. Doubtless she would not have welcomed publicity that rats, those unclean creatures, had attacked her.

I think it is sordidness, and years without the vitality that sunlight gives to the human body, that create the despair on which vice grows big in the large cities. It is known and often written, that in New York, in addition to many alcoholic men and women, there are a large number of drug addicts; and their numbers increase yearly, despite the strenuous attempts of the vice squad to end the traffic in those drugs that degrade and destroy human beings. How sad that the beautiful silken-white silver opium poppy, that superior nerve-soothing flower which once saved the life of my daughter Luz, when a doctor told me she would surely die, should be misused for commercial purposes. Sad, indeed, that it is turned into a highly destructive, addictive drug. Shimmering silver-white poppy beloved of me, I will ever protect you!

Like children playing at a game, a deadly game, drug addicts have a fancy language for their playthings. They talk about "a needle for a fix," or "a spike," about cocaine as "white stud," morphine as "junk."

"Grass," "jive," and "Mary Jane" are names for the popular marijuana, which is cheaper and readily obtainable in New York as it comes from nearby Mexico and South America.

I know musicians, composers, and artists who declare that they cannot work or face audiences without the help of marijuana; yet their hands, even when they are yet young in years, tremble like old men's, and they have the unpleasant pallor of the constipation that drug-taking brings with the destruction of the normal working ability of the intestinal nerves. One hears and sees warnings on American radio and television concerning the drug habit taking hold on New York's youth. And yet it is a fact that one very rarely finds drug-taking among the Gypsies: their frequent escape from the depression of city life, as they go off on their travels, may be one reason why they do not have to take drugs to make life seem more pleasant.

Drug-taking and allied human vices make human beings ugly. One sees ugly and unnatural human faces in the streets of big cities and one fears them. I always had to take my Afghan hound out into the street in the late night hours to cleanse herself before confining her for the night. The walk down the long, ill-lit stairs, out into the empty street with its bins, around which rats were sometimes seen, did not trouble me until one night of heavy rain when I was preparing the Afghan's bed by laying sheets of newspaper against her return, dripping with rain from the downpour, and an article on one of the pages caught my attention: It was called "Women in a Panic" and was the third in a series written by a police officer. The article warned women in New York of the dangers of nighttime streets. It warned that women should not be out alone after midnight, and that when their escorts take them home, it is not enough merely to take them to the house, but they should accompany the women up to their apartment doors, as danger may lurk in the passages of such places, or in deserted elevators. The article said that the stupid woman who walks her dog at night alone to the nearest plot of ground because she is ashamed for her dog to soil the sidewalks is inviting violence and rape. Keep the dog where it is safe, merely scoop up the excreta into a bag and put it in to a garbage bin.

Every night after I read that article, I went down the ill-lit stairs of the apartment building in fear! I regretted that I was not in the lands of the near world-conqueror Genghis Khan. For that ill-reputed, and so-called barbarian, ruler could boast that a virgin carrying a sack of gold could walk unescorted the length and breadth of his vast domains without any harm befalling her.

When later, the Messrs. Polo (of the Marco Polo family) escorted the beautiful seventeen-year-old virgin princess Kokachin, with much treasure, from the court of the great Khan, Kublai, the successor of Genghis, they were proving that his boast was true and still held good. For, unmolested, the company crossed the great domains of the Khan to deliver her as bride to King Arghun of the Levant.

A friend of mine, a beautiful young girl, Norma Jean Nielson, had once been a dancer in the famous New York club, the Copacabana, on East 60th Street, where visitors are able to see what is often described as "the loveliest line of chorus girls in New York City, in miniature review." She often had to leave the club unescorted when the show ended in the early hours of the morning. She feared going out alone into the New York streets. Therefore, to walk back to her apartment, some distance away, in safety, she would put on a disguise: She half hid her face in a wide Arab scarf, covered her eyes with horn-rimmed glasses, donned baggy trousers, and, with her feet in snowboots, shuffled through the New York streets!

My most frightening experience in New York, strangely enough, took place at the window of our apartment on Second Avenue, at the rear window, which looked onto 78th Street. I never thought to lower the blinds over our windows; I had lived so long in country places where one has never wanted to shut out the light of the moon and the stars!

The Gypsies divide the human race into two kinds: the People of the Roofs and the People of the Skies. They say that People of the Roofs prepare for the night by bolting their doors, closing their windows, and curtaining them against the night, whereas People of the Skies bed themselves on the ground beneath the sky and enjoy the moon and the stars. If they live in vans or tents, they always keep door and window open, or tent flaps lifted.

One February night, around midnight, I regretted that I had never thought to curtain our windows. The window facing ours at the rear was also uncurtained. I was sprinkling herbal powder along the base of the door to make sure that no cockroaches entered from outside, when my eyes were attracted to a fearful scene being enacted against the closed, facing window. Silhouetted there were a man and woman clasped in what looked to me like a death struggle. The man had his hands around the woman's throat, and her neck was being forced so far back that I thought it must surely break from her body, like the head from a flower. Not that there was anything flowerlike about her. Disheveled hair and a blown-out silhouette. I could see the woman more clearly than the man; he seemed merely slight of build and with a sparsely covered, small head. With the powder clutched in my hand, I stood there, too astonished to think much or to move at all, an unwilling spectator of a real-life horror scene.

I heard no cries, no screams. I saw the woman slip from between the man's hands, seemingly down onto the floor. She went out of my sight and I never saw her again.

Then my fears were intensified, for they became personal and cowardly. The window behind which the fight had been taking place was abruptly flung open, and the man stood there, watching me.

My window, too, was open. Being one of the People of the Skies, I kept my windows always open everywhere I went and often gained for myself the wrath of my hosts because they said that I froze their houses. Now the man looked across to me, from open window to open window. Only the short span of a flat roof separated us. Yet he remained a vague, spectral figure. Now that I had the opportunity to see him fully, I dared not look in his direction at all. I kept my own eyes lowered. I believed that he had a revolver in his hand! I felt sure of that, but I dared not look to lessen or increase my fears with what I should see.

The minutes went by. I never remember knowing such great terror. I think that the sordidness of the scene accounted for my state of mind. I have seen many frightening things on my travels. I have been in the midst of Gypsy tribe fights, where knives were used, and in skirmishes of the Arabs against the French in Oran. Once in London I was alone in a room with a mad workman who was taken to a lunatic asylum; I was once alone in a New York lift with an amorous lift operator; as a teenager, I was chased over lonely cliffs in Wales by an ugly soldier. In every case I had been frightened, but I had always escaped almost unharmed.

At the New York window I knew my fears were far greater than on any of the other unpleasant occasions. I well remember my feelings – how my heart drummed and my forehead pricked with sweat, and how I would not draw breath in case (and this must be how a crouching, hunted animal feels) I should attract more attention to my presence. How long the passing minutes seemed, how endless!

Then, as I stood petrified, a thought came to me, which was to pretend that I had not seen the man and woman fighting, and further that I was not aware of the man watching me and possibly pointing a gun at me.

I knew that I should have shut the windows and then raced for the door and brought help to the possibly dying or murdered victim of the man facing me, but nothing would have induced me to leave my children alone in the room within his reach, nor was I brave enough to go down those dark stairs and possibly meet the man waiting for me out in the street when I got there. I felt that as soon as I went to the door, the man would know that I was seeking police help and would shoot me instantly; and then also kill my sleeping children!

Therefore, as soon as the saving thought came to me, I began to sprinkle the insect powder – as I had intended to do when alarmed by the fight at the window. No revolver bullet came tearing across at me. I therefore went to the refrigerator and pretended to be doing things there. Then I unnecessarily turned on the bath taps. Still nothing happened from the facing window. Made bolder, I walked away and opened the door of the front room and called to my dog. She came to me at once. I wanted the man, still facing me at the window, to see that I had a large dog for protection. I then finally dared to step across to our apartment window, close it, and then for the first time since we had come there nearly three months ago, lower the window blind. Thus I shut out from my sight the terrifying man who had been facing me for what had seemed a very long time.

I then hurried to the front room, accompanied by my dog, and barricaded the door with a heavy table and many chairs. In the morning I would go to the police. There was no telephone in the apartment. Unfortunately, as had not been the case with the window cleaner who had stolen my purse and whose physical features I had noticed in great detail, I had been too afraid of the man at the window to look long enough at him to be able to describe him or even to recognize him if I should ever see him again. I only remembered paleness, the slight figure, and the balding, small head. That was all.

In the morning I went at once to my friends, Loretta and Hermine, in the shop below our apartment and told them what I had seen and asked their advice as to how I should contact the police. They are both wise young women, and they advised me not to go at first to the police at all but instead to visit the owner of the liquor shop above which the room where I had seen the fight was located, tell him what had occurred there, and ask him who occupied the room and what he thought I should do concerning the police.

Therefore I went to the liquor shop and spoke with the owner. His reply was unexpected. He told me that the room where I had seen the fighting – and all the other rooms of the building where he had his shop – were cheap lodging rooms let by the night, especially to middle-class types of people who were not the kind who usually went in for killing each other. Almost surely what I had seen was a drunken fight. The man had merely opened the window to get air and most probably had not even noticed me there facing him. He did not think the police would be interested in such a slight story. I accepted his advice, but I warned him that since I had told him what I had seen, and the affair was in his building, it was now his responsibility. Further, I said that one could forgive and pity a drunken crime or a crime of passion, but it would not be forgivable if that unpleasant-looking and brutal man, of whom I had got a vague impression, was making a habit of taking women to that room and treating them in the horrible way that I had witnessed.

I went away from the liquor shop wondering why human beings should choose to make their lives so ugly so often, to fill themselves with overmuch alcohol, and go to an unpleasant place and hope to capture the beauty of love in that manner; love is always so elusive. Better the love way of the birds of paradise, who dance before each other for hours before they mate. They dance in love bowers where they have cleared the ground and strewn brightly colored and sweetly perfumed leaves and flowers.

I put the matter of the window fight out of my mind, almost, following my talk with the store owner. Every night at dusk I covered the window with the window blind for fear that I should see again the horrible man's face staring across at me.

Then, one week after the incident, I noticed something peculiar about the window opposite. Two large-sized cartons of milk standing there on the right-hand corner of the sill were bursting their contents. I remembered then that I had seen them in exactly the same position, one a little forward from the other, but both touching, for an entire week, ever since I had witnessed the fighting. Now the cartons were bulging because the unused milk had soured and expanded and was pressing open the waxed sides. The thought then possessed me as to who had purchased the two large cartons of milk, expensive enough, and then failed to use them, leaving all that milk there to rot?

I decided forthwith to tell the police all that I had seen at the window opposite and to show them the cartons of milk. Once, years ago in the New Forest in England, when I had been living in a Gypsy van at Blissford in the forest, I had heard soon after dusk the frantic screams of a woman: "Help me! Help me!" she had screamed. I was less frightened in the familiar environment of a forest than I had been at a New York window. And I had risked leaving my children in charge of my Afghan hound while I ran to the nearest telephone, a good distance away, to bring the police to the scene. The police had come a while later and had found nothing.

As I was absolutely positive about hearing the frantic cry, the police concluded that I must have heard a vixen screaming, it being springtime. I refused to accept the police explanation – I knew I had heard a woman in great terror, screaming for help. The following morning I searched around for myself. In the exact distant field that I had indicated as the place of the cries, I found the wheel tracks of a car. Also on the boggy ground were the footprints of a man and a woman. I told the police and they searched again, but nothing further of the frightened woman was ever known.

The New York police frequently called on my friends in the shop below my apartment to drink coffee with them. I asked them to let me know when the next one came. They called me that same day, and I found myself with an Irish-American policeman. It was said in New York at that time that the Irish had the police force right in the family. Certainly nearly every policeman with whom I spoke answered me with a fine Irish brogue.

This policeman, when I told him my story of the fight at the window, said with humor, "You said this happened a week ago. Can't you smell the body yet across the roof?"

"That is for you to find out," I replied.

A short while afterwards, when I went out shopping, I saw the policeman standing in the rain there, in the street, facing the window that I had indicated to him. Chin on hand, a puzzled look on his face, he was studying the two milk cartons. By that evening the cartons had been removed.

I do not know what the police found. I was leaving for Mexico within a few days. Several times in those days I saw police cars driving down 78th Street. Possibly they always did and I was only aware of them now because I was interested.

Although the New York scene was often sordid, one of the blessings of that great city is its nearness to beautiful countryside. New York is a fair state. It is a place of apple orchards and bluebirds (the emblem bird of New York State). Within as little as an hour of driving, one can reach the quiet marshes and woods of Long Island.

Only a little farther away is Westchester, a place of beautiful gardens and far-stretching apple orchards, and an abundance of wildflowers and animals to be found there – including poison ivy!

Neighboring New Jersey and Connecticut are also within easy driving from New York City, and parts of both are rich in natural beauty. I had friends in all these places, and, like the nomadic Gypsies, we would escape from city life to where we could enjoy turf under our feet again, and above, the company of the sun by day, and the moon and the stars by night. Where we could glory in the monotonous, but longed-for, wind sounds, soughing through tree branches and stirring winter-dried leaves, grasses, and the bents [grass stalks] on the marshes.

The city of New York itself has some wild vegetation right within its gray concrete heart and apart from the monotonous grassy stretches of its parklands. Wherever there were empty lots awaiting the builders, the winds would bear seeds there, and those plants that could endure the impure air of cities and rank soil would sprout and grow up. I could see, when the snow melted on the city lots, fireweed and greater willow-herb – some of the first plants to take possession of cleared or burned land – also dandelion, stinging nettle, and goldenrod.

Whenever I see goldenrod I think of the Native American Indians. It was their flower! The prairie goldenrod would send the Indian braves back from their hunting camps to their women and children, for when the goldenrod turned its deepest gold they knew that their fields of corn would be ripe for harvesting, and also that the nuts would be ready for taking from the woods. Goldenrod is a natural compass, too. When growing in the open away from the shade of trees or bushes, it always points north. Furthermore, the Indians made a beautiful yellow dye from golden-

rod flowers; it was a favorite color for tinting their basketware. [Goldenrod is *Solidago.*]

Being a botanist and an herbalist, anything to do with wild plants is of much interest to me. The origin of the abundant wild plants found in New York State is as interesting to trace as any mystery in a thriller story. Many of New York State's wild plants are known to have come as seeds in the hay that various conquerors brought with them as fodder for their horses. Cortez and Pizarro and the Duke of York's men all brought horse hay when they came to America, as did the many Gypsy tribes. The Pilgrim Fathers brought seeds in the mud caked onto their farm tools and country clogs. There would also have been seeds in the horse fodder that the Hessians carried with them when they waged war against Washington's battalions. Thus, new wild plants, many bearing beautiful flowers, came to New York and to America.

A recent story concerning wild plants in the region adjoining New York also has a detective-story element in it. Some unusual foreign plants appeared in a Connecticut River valley. As none had ever before been seen in the locality, a botanist went there to investigate. After a long and careful search, the botanist found that a factory dealing in scrap rubber was the source of the foreign plants. In the factory yards were piles of old rubber footwear discarded by immigrants from many lands. From Russia and Poland and Canada, from Eire to the South Americas, the owners of these rubber galoshes and high boots had brought foreign plant seeds in the mud clinging to their soles. Rains had then washed the mud from the rubber heaps in the factory's yards, and the seeds therein had further been carried down the Connecticut River, to root there and flower along its banks.

A Gypsy herbalist of the Pyrenees

Chapter Seven

Last Winter in New York

For our return and last visit to New York, we went to another friend's apartment, this time in Washington Place, behind Washington Square, in Greenwich Village. We were in the land of the hatters: most of the surrounding buildings were being used by old established firms manufacturing headgear. Vans departed laden with boxed hats, or piled pyramids of them.

It was also the locality of New York University. We walked the nearby streets in the company of crowds of students. They seemed to be of all nationalities, and they dressed in a more informal way than I had seen students dress in other cities, even including Paris.

The winter weather was cold, and most of the young women were therefore in trousers; only painted faces do not match well with trousers and made many of the young women look like ventriloquists' dolls. The many Indian women students endured the cold in their thin silk saris, with only a warmer topcoat above, but leaving their knees and ankles sparsely clad.

Everyone seemed happy, and one did not feel that strain and tension of survival that I myself have experienced when I studied at two European universities.

My children and I liked the Washington Square area. There were more trees, and the sky was more open. Moonlight actually flooded in through our open windows at nights. One could lie in bed and hear river music, for we were between Manhattan's two great rivers.

The music was of ship sirens and the bark of the foghorns, which came low and urgent and was like the calling of gray seals. I liked the misty nights when the foghorn was warning through all the hours of darkness until the coming of the light of the mornings.

The history of old New York told us that Washington Place was once a potter's field, and a place where criminals were hanged in public. The whole of Greenwich Village had once been a secluded rural spot, until a smallpox epidemic spread through New York in 1793, and caused a large migration of frightened people to that healthful country village.

More than anywhere else in New York, one has an impression in the village of time for "recollecting in tranquility." There are houses made beautiful by age, old winding passages, rare woodwork carved by the skilled hands of careful craftsmen of older times – carved doors and wall panels and beautiful balustrades in the houses.

Bleecker Street presented a strange contrast with other parts of New York; it seemed more European, with its merchandise piled on the stalls outside the shops. And there were unusual foods to be seen: pine cones, fennel hearts, foreign things in strange baskets and bags. Chestnut sellers, usually of African heritages, passed by with their trays of fragrant nuts. We even met a Spanish seller of sweet Carolina potatoes, and an Italian roasted peanut vendor. These people shouted their wares in foreign accents, the only street cries that I ever heard in New York.

Once in New York the street vendors had been numerous and their cries had been music in the streets. I wish I could have heard them all. There had been the sellers of boiled corncobs, crying "Corn-oh! Golden corn!" And other sellers crying, "Baked pears!" "Sweet potatoes! Carolina potatoes!" "Clams, oysters, fresh! Sea fresh!" "Milk-oh!" (from wooden cans on yokes). "Fresh strawberries! Fresh blackberries!" "Fresh-picked nuts!" "Fresh tea rusks" "Sand! Sand! Lily-white sand!" And the little chimney-sweepers, mostly young Black men, also went by crying shrilly, "Chimerneys to sweep kl-ee-n! Kl-ee-n! Kl-ee-n!" They were all around in New York City, as late as in the nineteen-twenties. [And some are still there, even now.]

It was very cold during the time that we were in the Village, and all along Bleecker Street the store owners would light big fires in their refuse bins: old fruit boxes and suchlike were burned there in the evening when the weather turned coldest, and it was fun to walk down the street with firelight flickering and the scent of burning wood on the air, that scent which every Gypsy loves.

The Village has been called the Gypsydom of New York, but I never saw any true Romanies there. Romany Marie, a famed and beloved Village character, had gone away years ago. Once the village was populated largely by artists, writers, and musicians who went to live there, not only to be among their own kind, which is always pleasant, but also because then in Greenwich Village: "Those needful of a place to sleep, Came here because the rents were cheap."

There is still an active art colony there. A song composer friend, Jack Jones, told me of the days when musicians and others would rent one room in the village, cheaply, as a studio, without hot water or sanitation. But they would sleep in the room also, on bedrolls on the floor as the Gypsies do, hastily putting them out of the way if the landlord was likely to be coming around.

The house that interested me most in the Village was numbered 75½ Bedford Street and was only nine and a half feet wide and thirty feet deep – supposedly the narrowest house in New York. But more interesting than the size of the house was the fact that in it a poetess had lived whose work I love greatly, Edna St. Vincent Millay. Her poetry has singing in it always.

> What lips my lips have kissed, and where and why,
> I have forgotten, and what arms have lain
> Under my head till morning; but the rain
> Is full of ghosts tonight. . . .

There were artists as well as poets in the Village, and the artists seemed hard at work. Often as we walked in the Village we saw young men and women coming out of houses carrying unframed paintings in their arms, the paint looking scarcely dry. We peered and then asked if we could see the paintings. Many of them were very good: imaginative subjects mostly, though sometimes portraits of the Village youth, especially the disheveled-headed beatniks, and also of some local scenes.

Parties were a feature of Village life. Held in lofts and basements often enough, and with the true spirit of Bohemia. People say that the carefree spirit has departed from Greenwich Village life and that what is left is mere pretense. I did not find that true at all!

What singing of the blues by the Blacks at the parties! Nothing better, not even from the professionals on records or the radio. Sometimes a Gypsy came along to strum a guitar. The music was often fantastic: Everything was used. Never before had I known that matches shaken in half-empty boxes could make loud and dramatic music. That strange rhythmical ticking produced a sound not unlike the rattle of a rattlesnake's tail, which I had become familiar with in California.

Some of the young Village women could boast powerful and really passionate voices; many of them wore no makeup, and their hair, often blonde, hung in long, thick, goose-girl plaits over one shoulder.

Rock'n'roll was still being danced; the "twist" had not yet become the rage. One of the people I remember best from Village parties was Adrienne Adler, a sweet-faced singer of ballads. Her voice was also sweet, with something of the sadness of skylarks in it. Although larks are considered to be joyous birds, I do not think that this is so, for they leave their song in the sky and drop in silence back to earth.

I shall long remember her ballads, accompanied by her own, very old, hand-carved American guitar, rising above the party hum. The song, by Pete Seeger, for which she was most asked was *Where Have All the Flowers Gone*? This song was popular in the sixties. I thought it truly described the life of man. The ballad laments that the young maids have gone to the young men, and the young men have become soldiers, and the soldiers are in their graves and the graveyards are crowded with flowers, and the flowers, of course, are in the hands of the young maids. And it ends: "When will they ever learn? When will they ever learn?"

That last winter, we hastened back to New York City for Christmas, knowing how wonderful it is there, especially in the village. Our hound, Cingane, had been left behind on Long Island to have puppies, and we had with us instead a gray male Afghan puppy, Esparto-grass. We were to arrive on Christmas Eve in time to have a few hours with our friend Betty Butterworth, a true Bohemian, who was kindly lending us her apartment in the Village while she traveled in Europe. We traveled from Mexico to Los Angeles, thence to Chicago, where we had to change trains for New York.

In Chicago we refused to travel on the train we were booked on because the baggage car had been taken off, and we would not let our dog travel alone on the later train without us there to take care of him, though the railway officials suggested – almost insisted – that we do so.

The railway clerks were cynical about our refusal, saying that we must love animals very much. We do love animals very much! I was still feeling sad and angry about the death of a steer on the Mexico–California border and carried the newspaper clipping around with me concerning its death.

The clipping was from the *San Diego Times*, and this is what happened: A steer escaped from a Tijuana, Baja California, slaughterhouse, when a hammer blow had proved insufficient to kill it. The eight-hundred-pound animal, maddened by the pain of the blow, ran across the border into San Ysidro. There he met with a score of children leaving the San Ysidro Catholic Academy. A police sergeant, E.C. Stevens, reported that one boy was directly in the path of the charging animal. The youngster escaped unhurt when he fell and the steer ran over him without touching him.

The steer had come across the international border running at a reported thirty-five miles an hour – "wild and deadly." Yet the animal had stepped over a fallen child! The steer was eventually caught and returned to the meat-packing house for slaughter, yes, for slaughter, after a check by a U.S. Department of Agriculture veterinarian.

But the animal had spared the life of a human child! Surely it should have been given a garland of laurel leaves and been pensioned off to graze on some pleasant pasture for the rest of its life. Instead, it was returned to be slaughtered in the same place that had so terrified its heart a few hours before. Have human beings no mercy, no compassion for those sentient creatures they merely classify as meat?

This is not the first time that a stampeding cow or bull has spared the life of a human child. I write with feeling because my own boy, when two years old, was in the path of a stampeding cow running from a butcher in the Sierra Nevada mountains in Spain. A miller of Lanjaron witnessed this. There seemed no hope for Rafik. He would either be knocked by the animal into a bordering stream and crush his head on the rocks there, or be trampled underfoot. The cow stopped when she reached the child, sniffed at him, stepped carefully over, and then rushed onwards! [Read this story in *Spanish Mountain Life*, Ash Tree Publishing.]

Telling my children about the incident of the steer, and how Rafik had himself once been saved by such an animal, my six-year-old daughter, Luz, said, "If I were Queen of the World, and Rafik were King, we would not let anyone frighten or hurt any animal. I would make laws!"

In all my books I have purposely mentioned animals and pleaded for their rights in the world.

A well-known Catholic, Archbishop Ambrose Agius, wrote, in 1937, that a great new worldwide interest was being taken in the rights of animals. Is it because great numbers of people, as we came to discover, were resentful of the current cynicism with regard to animals: the attitude that they have no souls, and no rights, and therefore – oh devastating illogicality – we can treat them as we like? Or is it because we are sickened at the cruelty of human towards human? Or is it because human instinct refuses to accept a double standard: consideration for humankind and remorseless savagery for animals?

Anyway, if we had let our Afghan hound travel alone on that late evening train from Chicago, we would have collected a dead dog in New York the following day. He would have been frozen to death; for, as it happened, that very train – and we were on it along with our dog – became snowbound and arrived in New York seven hours and forty-five minutes late.

The Pennsylvania Railroad train, the Manhattan Express, was stuck outside Pittsburgh in subzero weather when the diesel engine failed through lack of fuel. The train's plight was reported on the New York radio, and the next day I read about our journey on the Manhattan Express on the front page of *The New York Times*!

The baggage car, where I had to put the puppy in his wooden crate, leaked snow. It piled up on the luggage stacked there. The car also bucked like a wild horse, crashing the dog up against the roof of his crate. The cold of the subzero weather was intense in that car; I spent hours with Espartograss, unable to let him endure such painful transport alone. At last, when the train was stranded in the snow and conditions in the baggage car truly became impossible, the guard granted my request to have the dog with us in the passenger car.

This extraordinary Christmas journey to New York was made all the more dramatic because I became involved in my first public brawl. If it was cold in the baggage car, it was unbearably hot in our passenger car.

As proof of the heat, when I later took the Afghan hound's temperature to see if the terrible journey had made him ill, the thermometer registered 108 degrees Farenheit. This temperature, I was relieved to find, was not caused by a fever that the dog had developed, but by the heat of the railway carriage which had sent the mercury soaring as the thermometer lay in my handbag. Also a loaf of homemade whole wheat bread, which the ranch had given us to eat on the journey, exploded when I began to cut it open, caused by the fermentation that the heat had generated within the loaf. The steaming bread had to be tossed into the snow along the railway track, how sad. Its natural ingredients would have made healthful and delicious eating during that travel ordeal.

There were several dozen people gathered in the compartment during the many hours that the train was snowbound, and not one window could open. The air-conditioning was not working – as usual on American air-conditioned trains (and ships) on which I have traveled.

For part of the journey, a very pleasant family was seated near us; they said they came from near the Canadian border. They, too, deplored the heat of the carriage, and between us we kept the door open all the time of their journey and thus enjoyed the entry of some reviving fresh air.

Then, when the fresh-air-loving family left the train, a large dark woman moved her luggage over to their place, closed the door with angry force, seated herself alongside me, and kept protesting to me that my dog was looking at her. From the moment this woman arrived, each time I opened the door to let in some clean air, she glared at me or shook her fist at me. Eventually she said she would "attack" me if I dared to open the door again.

When my children and dog were all three panting with the airless, intense heat, and the children pleading, "We'll die! We'll die! It's so hot!" I returned to the door and opened it. The attack came, and with fury! The woman rose from her seat and, like a black bull, rushed at me.

She grasped my blouse, trying to tear it off me. She seemed an experienced fighter! I did not fight back. I stood there, letting her do all the attacking. When she pulled my hair, my children and the other people nearby began to shout at her. She took her hands off me and went back to her seat. She said: "If you dare touch that door again, I'll kill you!"

I replied: "I will not attack you, nor kill you, but I'll write about you in a book!"

I sat down and took pencil and paper and described her, then read it to her so her own ears could hear. I ended my description by telling her that she had achieved a record in my experience, that never before had I seen a person able to do what she could do, and that was that she "chewed gum, smoked a cigarette, and ate food, all at the same time – a nasty mixture of gum, smoke, and meat sandwiches!"

The intervals came when our neighbor in the train snored with her mouth open. Then the door would be flung wide open, by me. The good, cool, fresh air, coming in often awakened her, but she did not attack me again. So the unpleasant journey was passed, and was forgotten in the joy of Christmas in New York, which began the following day.

Christmas is wonderful in all the big cities of the world, where it is celebrated through the pleasure of theater, pantomime, and the decorated shop windows, apart from the many friends with whom to share the pleasures. I have never seen more splendid shop windows in any city than those along Manhattan's Fifth Avenue. Visiting them was like taking my children to a fantastic theater. The sky was tinted the pink of sea coral over New York with the increased blaze of special Christmas lights. There were snow-feathers in the air blowing over the lights, and the snow when it turned to sleet fell down in silver plaits over the glittering scene. A poet described such lights:

> Lights are silence singing and lights are choirs.

Certainly the flash and sparkle were silent, but they mimed powerfully the spirit of Christmas, which was felt everywhere. The Jews of New York, though many of them did not believe in the miraculous birth of the Christ child, which their city was celebrating, feted the Christmas as wholeheartedly as the believers. The great Jewish-owned shops along Fifth Avenue and Broadway were foremost in the brilliance of their Christmas lights, and also the artistic beauty of their decorations.

One Christmas in Paris, my children and I had seen an unforgettable window display in a clothing shop on Avenue Victor Hugo. It was the whole play of Cinderella, enacted by dolls moved by electricity. During our second Christmas in New York, we were to see a Manhattan window display at Altman's, on Fifth Avenue, which was the loveliest of all. Called "An Old-Fashioned Christmas in Town and Country," it showed window after window of moving toy children, and animals accompanying them, especially a family of dressed mice who skated, prepared Christmas dishes, danced, and so forth. At every window there stood a crowd of admiring and delighted children and adults. We stood among them; we were witnessing a magical sight.

The fountains of the city were illuminated, and countless apartment windows were individually decorated with colored lights, holly wreaths, and flashing stars of Bethlehem. A great cross of lights shone over the city, formed by specially illuminated windows of the Grand Central Station tower.

By tradition, established in 1933, a giant spruce tree shines above Rockefeller Center, tossing its green, light-strung boughs below high office windows of the buildings. A miniature forest of one hundred and fifty balsam trees from Canada, decorated with fifteen thousand lights, is displayed at the Seagram building on Park Avenue, which avenue is among the most beautiful in New York.

On our second Christmas, now that we had come to know the Gypsies of New York, we were invited to many Gypsy homes. All the Gypsies were wearing magnificent new clothes and showing wonderful jewelry, which flashed like the Christmas lights of the city. In all their homes they were feasting on turkey and sweet potatoes and chestnuts. And there was good wine; wine is the blood of the traveling people, the Gypsies say. There was Gypsy singing. Gypsy carols are beautiful. They have been called profane. I found them simple and sweet, like children's made-up songs.

I shall remember my Christmas visit to Madame Star's (Maria Niccolovitch's) place on Houston Street because there was a great company of Gypsy men there instead of the usual gathering of women in the fortune-telling *ofisas*. The men were very excited about my collection of Gypsy photographs, which I had lent to the family, especially as they recognized some Hungarian cousins in a photograph I had taken at the Gypsy fiesta of Les Saintes Maries de la Mer, in France.

They were all visiting for Christmas, from Los Angeles, and they began telling me about the King of the Gypsies there, how he had absolute control over the Gypsy trades in the city, and further had the right to any of the Gypsy women, even when they were married women.

One man, named Mark, told me that the king had claimed his young wife for three weeks, instead of the few days that he usually kept the Gypsy women, and that ever since she had been hostile to him, her rightful husband, and vain because the king had kept her so long, and she wanted to return to him, "the massive, powerful man," as she called him.

Three Gypsy gentlemen of Granada:
mule-trader (with clippers), singer, field-worker

All the other men agreed that the king had such rights. It was surprising, considering the known strict morals of Gypsy women, one basic reason for the survival and strength of the Gypsy race.

The Los Angeles king had a brother in New York who also had great power over nearly all the Gypsy tribes there, apart from the true country nomads who came to the city sometimes, and whom the other, more prosperous Gypsies contemptuously called "rag-heads." Only the king's brother in New York did not interfere with the Gypsy women.

I was told that the King of the Gypsies came to New York Hospital's General Medical Center for treatment, and that he did not bring any women with him, but a large bodyguard of hefty men, who caused some problems for the hospital staff. But all ended well.

Many friends came with me to Madame Star's and Caterina Markovitch's homes, and all commented on the good manners of the Gypsy children. Out in the streets the Gypsy children may have been little begging nuisances, but in their homes they were admirable. In the New York *ofisas* the little boys were mostly busy playing cards and the little girls with their dolls, but all showed courtesy to the visitors and absolute obedience to their parents. Gareen Shay, a fair-haired model friend of mine, who went around New York dressed in black and leading a black Afghan hound, visited Gypsy families many times with me. To help the Gypsies, we distributed their fortune-telling advertisement bills for them among our friends.

These made strange reading. There must be some printer in New York making a good living from composing and printing these advertisement sheets. The composer does not seem a well-educated person! Perhaps it is a Gypsy doing them on a hand printing-press! They are all similar, although the contents are all different. There is humor in them, though not intended humor.

Madame Star's bill read:

> Reader, Adviser & Healer. Don't Classify Her with Gypsies. If you're unhappy, discouraged, in sorrow, if you lost someone dear to you, don't fail to see this Gifted Lady Today. Tomorrow may be too late. Upon reaching womanhood and realizing she had the God-given power to help humanity, she has devoted a lifetime to this work. From the four corners of the world they come to her. Guaranteed to remove evil influences and bad luck. She invites you to her house. Speaks seven languages including Spanish. (Address, telephone number.) Reading Half-Price with this Ad.

"Invites you to her house!" Her "house" was a ground-floor room in the Bowery. She herself was very proud of her Gypsy race and thought and lived like the true Gypsy that she was. The ad was obviously written for her, and she had to take what the printer decided was to be said.

Madame Valiant's (my friend Mary Williams's) bill said:

> Results guaranteed. Astrology Reader & Advisor. If you are sick, worried, in need of help. See The Psychic Lady. Will tell you anything you wish to know without asking any questions. . . If worried, troubled or in doubt, consult this gifted lady at once. She can and will help you. Gives help and advice on business, love, marriage and speculations of all kinds. She does what others claim to do. One visit will convince you she is different and superior to all others you have consulted. All readings Private and strictly confidential. (Address, phone.) Reading Half-Price with this ad.

Then there was Sister Eve's bill:

> Spiritual Reader and Advisor was born with the God-given powers to help humanity & has devoted her life to this work. Tell your friends' and enemies' names without asking a single word. . . .Will give Lucky Hands & Charms. No problem so great that she can't solve. . . . She removes evil influences and bad luck of all kinds. She never fails to reunite the separated, cause speedy & happy marriages. . . . You will find her superior to any other reader

> you have consulted in the past. A place to bring your friends and feel no embarrassment. Address: One flight up (telephone). Reading half-price with this ad.

I went to visit Sister Eve and her "place to bring your friends and feel no embarrassment." And I went with friends, as she suggested – friends who had never before met Gypsies! We took cakes and wine with us, prepared to have a good time. But her place was empty. That usual Gypsy flitting!

From there, we went to the Gypsy hand-reading parlor of Mary Illynavitch Williams. I have seldom seen anyone who looked less like her humble name than that flashy, powerful, but truly talented Gypsy. But alas, when we reached her place, we found it shuttered and empty, with only her name in white paint still on the windows.

It was again as Rachel Field, poetess, wrote concerning the American Gypsies in her book *The Painted People*:

> All gone away,
> Who knows where. . . .
>
> Never a shaggy Gypsy dog,
> Never a Gypsy child,
> Only a burnt-out Gypsy fire,
> Where danced that band so wild.

So I took my friends instead to the curio shop of the Armenian, which was below the Williams' former apartment, the one I described earlier. The Gypsies danced outside his mother's window at the time of his birth in a Turkish village. He might be able to give us news of Mary.

I wanted to copy (for this book) some of the ridiculous words printed on the "crying towels" at the curio shop. They were illustrated in bright prints with cartoon-like characters, and were supposed to be thrust at irate, tired, or grumbling members of one's family. I saw towels for father and mother, father-in-law and mother-in-law, husband and wife, fishermen, golfers, and so forth – all so exceedingly vulgar and insane that I wondered how anyone could ever want to spend money on such. There were also stupid texts, in plain wooden frames meant to resemble religious texts. One said simply, "I like Sex." Curious as to who would buy such things, I asked the Armenian, who told me that he sold large numbers to "college people."

On this visit all the towels and texts had gone. All had been sold, I was informed, but he was expecting more and would keep some for me if I wished. I replied that I was not a buyer and had only wanted to copy down the words on the towels as an example of modern progress. My friends said that, for the sake of America's good reputation, it was a good thing that there were no towels in the shop to provide me with copy for my book.

The Armenian told us that Esther Williams had left soon after my last visit to his place, during my former stay in New York, and that he had not seen her in the district since. But there was "someone else" of the Gypsy world just along the avenue, going right. He accompanied us to the door and indicated the place, and that way we came to Sister Eve's *ofisa* on a first floor, midway down Lexington Avenue. It is a superior address – she must have done well at her former place.

The advertising bill had been correct as to Sister Eve's having a good type of *ofisa.* It was well furnished and spacious and in quiet taste. Here were none of those curtained, cupboard-like places, those little puppet-theaters of Gypsy magic, as they have been called, but a pleasant apartment, the only indication that it was the place of a professional fortune-teller being the Signs of the Zodiac, large in size, well painted, across the wall facing the entry door.

A smartly dressed, good-looking Gypsy boy opened the door to us. At his heels was a stylish Boston terrier puppy. "A Christmas present from my mother," he told me.

He called to his mother, and Sister Eve came to us.

Sister Eve was a good-looking, youngish, typical Gypsy woman, notable for her proudly carried, beautiful neck, adorned with many necklaces of that dark red coral favored by Madame Prince, and also with pearls.

I was pleased that my friends were meeting such an attractive representative of the Gypsy race. Most of the American Gypsies I have seen are handsome, especially the Serb and Romanian Gypsy women, who are often strikingly beautiful. But there are some, whom I have met in New York and Chicago, with the faces and ways of vultures.

The Gypsy brought chairs for us and then sat down facing us. One member of our party, with the good sense of

Barefoot Gypsies; Spain

humor typical of him, introduced me to Sister Eve as "Sister Juliette." We sat and talked about American Gypsies. Eve said that she knew Esther and had seen her and her good-looking daughter at a recent big Gypsy feast of Saint Agatha. There were often big Gypsy feasts held in New York. The greatest of them all was held in June, associated with Saint Mary, and perhaps linked with the Corpus Christi Spanish celebrations of the same time.

Eve said she was American-born and very happy in America. She took pride in fortune-telling and really believed that she had gifts in this sphere.

I was holding a bag of herbs in my hand. They were a tea made from wildflowers, and I was taking them to a friend. The Gypsy noticed the herbs at once and asked to examine them. She said it seemed a wonderful herbal mixture, and she knew that the tea would be good for the nerves. That was true. She spoke with a knowledge of herbs, I could tell, and therefore I gave her some of the floral tea, telling her, truthfully, that it was based on an old Gypsy formula.

We shared our cakes and wine; the boy and his Boston terrier joined us. The boy proved to be very entertaining and was admirably fluent in Romany.

We then talked about Gypsy jewelry, and she commented on the big Arab earrings that I was wearing; she said that she feared they would split my earlobes. She showed us one of her ears with a scar down the lobe, where one of her children had once caught hold of one of her earrings and torn her ear through.

She was wearing gold-coin earrings, similar to those worn by many Gypsies in New York. They are made especially for the Gypsies by a Jewish jeweler in the Bowery. That special catering to the Gypsies reminded me of a Jewish tailor in Stepney, in London's East End, who specializes in making aprons for the English Gypsy women, plain aprons and fancy, but all with the big inside front pocket going right across the apron in typical Gypsy style, and big enough to hold a rabbit or a chicken!

While we sat talking with Eve, an aged, gray-haired Negro with metal-rimmed glasses worn low down on her nose came in for a hand reading. She sat nervously on the edge of the chair to which she had been shown, waiting for our conversation to finish and her hand reading to begin, her journey into the world of prophesying and magic. Not to keep the old woman waiting, we soon ended our conversation and left.

My friends found it a comedy: the old lady waiting so anxiously and with such determination to consult the Gypsy fortune-teller. Only they agreed with me that Sister Eve was both charming and beautiful and a good example of the interesting Gypsies of New York.

When later I went to visit the Gypsy artist painter Jan Yoors in his Manhattan studio by the river, nearly opposite the United Nations building, he shared this same opinion as to most of the American Gypsies.

"But," Jan Yoors said, "the Gypsies are the same all over the world really, interesting and charming people. Only the Spanish and English Gypsies differ from all the others, as if they had originated from some different Gypsy region."

It is true what Jan Yoors states about the English Gypsies. Many of those whom one meets there in the New Forest (now sadly confined to the compounds or Gypsy Reservations), and along the border counties approaching Scotland, and again many Gypsies found in Wales, look very different from the majority of the Gypsies of the world: they look more "Indian." The Spanish Gypsies are different again, and while their wailing and thrilling Flamenco singing bears more resemblance to Arab Moors, their carefully kept verbal pedigrees prove that they have seldom intermarried.

A Gypsy in New York

I had long wanted to meet Jan Yoors, ever since reading his series of articles – *O Drom Le Lowarengo* in the January-April 1961 issues of the *Journal of the Gypsy Lore Society*, founded in 1888 and located at Liverpool University, England – on his travels with the Lowara Gypsies, many of whom now live in, or pass through New York. My Spanish Gypsy article on life with the Gypsies at the horse fairs of Andalucia was also in the same issue of the *Journal*. Jan's article concluded his series. It began:

> The heavy wagons are lined up a few feet off the road and on both sides of it. The small fires are lit on the spaces left open between the wagons. We rattle past the first few fires before we realize that this is the camp. With an effort we stop the skittish horse on the spot and look around slightly dazed as if just waking from a strange dream. Some men pick up burning sticks, poke the fires to make them flare up, and holding burning pieces of wood high above their heads, and shading their eyes with the other hand to pierce the darkness, step forward to identify us. . . .
>
> Loudly we shout the customary exchange of greetings fit for the present and similar occasions, starting with *'Na daran, Rom sam wi ame'* ('Do not fear, we too are Gypsies' – the 'do not fear' meaning nothing more nor less, in fact, than a friendly interpolation). Out of the darkness many men's voices shout *'Develesa avilan'* ('With God you came'), to which we shout back, *'Develesa ara klam tume'* ('It is by the help of God himself that we have found you').
>
> We follow the torch-bearing men to a campfire, a little farther down the road. . . .

And so on. Fascinating reading! The Gypsies greet each other the same way when they meet in New York.

The *Journal* reached me in New York. Soon after I met the interesting Sally Gram Swing at the United Nations; because she thought I was typical of the Gypsies, she told me that she knew an artist who had lived with the Gypsies and would introduce me to him. I was delighted when she said his name was Jan Yoors.

Jan had been closer to the Gypsies than merely living with them. The Lowarengo adopted him (not stole him, as with Bee Bogen), and he lived and traveled with them for much of his life and speaks their language as one of his first languages.

Jan's studio was one of the nicest places that I visited while in New York: Huge and airy, with the river winds against the windows. There one did not slowly suffocate as in the modern Manhattan apartment houses. I found not only interesting paintings at Jan's place but also large tapestries, in which he specializes and has sold to many of America's greatest galleries.

The work of his that I wanted most to own merely showed an immense silver Gypsy moon against a thicket of crimson wands of leafless thorn trees. It was shown as a Gypsy would paint it: the silver moon and the thorns as seen by a man lying on the ground.

Jan said that he found New York an inspiring place in which to work, and therefore his work had prospered there. He said further that nearly everyone interesting in the world comes to New York at some point in their lives. The city today is especially a magnet for the artists and true Bohemians, Gypsies and non-Gypsies, and all who crave personal freedom in their lives.

French Gypsy basket- and chair-makers;
Les Saintes Maries de la Mer.

Chapter Eight

Goodbye to the New York Gypsies

As I was going away from New York soon, and as it is travelers among the Gypsies who attract me most, before leaving I was determined to try and find a certain Gypsy granny, relative of the Serbian Borrovitch Gypsy family from near Delancey Street, whom I had come to know. They told me that the grandmother, after her husband's death, had once traveled the whole of North and South America alone, in a mule-driven buggy cart, accompanied by a green parrot; and that she knew much about Gypsy life. An address in Brooklyn was described to me. But snowstorms and general bad weather delayed my visit almost until the time that I was due to leave New York. Then, with Bo Shay, who knows Brooklyn well, and his daughter Gareen, and, as usual, my two children, we set off for the Brooklyn locality described to us. Only it proved again that once more I was searching for Gypsies in vain in New York. My children still call futile quests "like searching for the Gypsy Granny in Brooklyn."

We had not waited for good weather, and it was snowing and almost below zero, and we searched six hours before I would give up! The only indication that there had been any Gypsies in the area were the words "Sister Anna,

Readings. Se habla Español" ill-written in white paint across the grimed window of an empty shop.

Only at the end of our search, we came across someone else who was not even dreamed of when we undertook our journey to Brooklyn. New York is like that, with the unexpected around almost every corner.

We were preparing to return to Manhattan when I saw a small shop, the window of which was filled with paintings. I felt instinctively that if there were any Gypsies around, they would visit such a place.

Bo wanted to enter also. An amateur artist himself, and with American Indian blood, the lurid colors of the paintings displayed attracted him. So we knocked on the door, and a man's voice told us not to go away but to wait for him. It seemed a strange greeting, but we waited.

Soon we heard the sound of wheels within the shop, and then, after some fumbling, the door was opened and a voice called to us, "Enter. Come in with you!"

We saw at the front of the shop, which was draped inside with curtains like a Gypsy *ofisa*, a gaunt, pale man seated in a wheelchair, which he propelled along with his own hands. He introduced himself, "Paul Haggenborg."

He told us that he was afflicted with arthritis in his legs and that he was completely crippled, unable to walk, but through need and will power he managed for himself. He was trying to make enough money with his paintings to pay for a journey to San Francisco, where he felt that the sunlight of the Golden City would cure him. He had had a vision concerning this. He knew the exact price of the fare, which had to include payment for an attendant, as the air companies would not take him otherwise, he being a helpless cripple.

I wished that I had had the money for his fare to San Francisco! He told us about his paintings. They were Psychic Paintings – that is what he called them. He merely put various colors on to board or canvas, and with his spirit directed the flow of the painting. The paintings were done in a form of trance. He had sent some of the best examples of his work to New York's Metropolitan Museum of Art, but they had been returned to him, as apparently they did not understand Psychic Paintings. We told him that we liked his unusual colorings, which were Gypsy-like and primitive. I asked him then if he knew the old Gypsy granny with the parrot who lived in that part of Brooklyn.

He informed me that he did not know of her, but that the Gypsies often came to visit him and inquire after his health. They just came by to talk with him and to cheer him up, and they shared their cigarettes with him. He loved them! Most artists love the Gypsies for their kind hearts and their gaiety, and the personal color that they daub across a too often drab modern world.

Paul told us about a woman who had come into his shop one day. She might have been a Gypsy, he did not know. From his description of her, the thought came to me that it might have been my Gypsy friend Madame Prince herself! Well, the woman came into his shop and brought with her a little pot that she told him contained scented oils, and said that she had come to cure him of his lameness. She would rub the oils into his feet, and he would be able to get up from his wheelchair and walk. He agreed to let his strange visitor use her oils on him, and she herself took off his boots and socks and then rubbed the oils into his feet and around his ankles. Soon his flesh began to tingle with life.

When he told the woman this, she rose up from the floor where she had been kneeling and, flinging out her arms like a cross, cried dramatically, "Now leave that chair and walk! Walk! Walk!"

Paul Haggenborg told us that then, to his astonishment, he had stepped down from his chair and walked! His first steps in years. Only the cure had not been lasting. The woman went away, and his strength began to wane. Only his legs remained in much better health than they had been since he had become crippled, and before her coming. Also, he felt happier. It had been a wonderful experience, the strange woman coming to him like that, with her scented oils and her kindness. The woman had come to him as a stranger and had left as a stranger, and he had never seen her again. It seemed to me very much the pattern of the Gypsy, the mysterious coming and going.

We began to talk about herbs. Bo believed in them, and I believed in them, and I was pleased that Paul Haggenborg believed also. I told the sick man to drink a tea of rosemary. The iron-rich blue flowers and steel-gray leaves denoted the nerve-tonic properties of the plant, a favorite with Mediterranean peasants and Gypsies through the ages. And rosemary is also famed as a heart tonic. I have cured the weakened hearts of racehorses with rosemary: one such horse was owned by the celebrated dance-band conductor Ambrose of England. After the treatment, that horse won races. Gypsies hang bunches of rosemary by the beds of their children to protect them from night fears and bad dreams, or rosemary is put under pillows.

Paul told us of his own experience with herbs, apart from these oils, which had surely been of herbal origin. He said that at the start of the sickness in his legs, his limbs had commenced such an uncontrollable twitching that he had had to go into the hospital. There in the hospital it had been impossible to keep any bedclothes on his bed because his twitching legs had kicked everything onto the floor. Then they had tried strapping him down, but that had made him feel very ill.

There was a Mexican doctor training at that New York hospital, and the doctor came to him one day and said that he would like to try one of his own people's remedies to allay the leg trouble. He said that he was giving the treatment without the authority of the hospital, which would not approve of all the herbal medicines of his own Aztec people. He had found unreasonable hostility to herbal medicine in North America; and this has been my own experience in my herbal veterinary work. He had said that the basis of the hostility was jealousy.

The remedy was a tea of the flowers of the passion plant (*Passiflora*), and he had to drink it, in secret, three times daily. After a short while, all the shaking had left his limbs, and the unpleasant trouble had never returned to increase the difficulties of his arthritic condition. The passion plant, named after Christ's passion, His death on the cross, is said to have grown from the tears of the Holy Mother Mary, weeping by the cross to which was nailed her wondrous son. This plant is only rivaled by the white opium poppy as a soother of pain and calmer of derangement.

I told Paul Haggenborg that he could surely get rosemary herb, and possibly passion plant blossoms also, from most Puerto Rican drugstores and the Latin-American botanicas in New York's Spanish Harlem. The latter were a good source of inexpensive herbal remedies that replaced the former famed medicinal herbs of the American Indians.

We wished Paul Haggenborg God's help in achieving his journey to San Francisco, and we left some money for the purchase of the two herbs. Then we went away from Brooklyn without finding the old Gypsy woman whom I sought.

It is really impossible to follow Gypsy trails, and it is more difficult in a vast and crowded place like New York than it is, for example, across the great range of the Sierra Nevada mountains of Spain's Andalusia, where I often searched for special Gypsy people whom I wanted to get to know – and usually found them.

When the Gypsies travel as nomads, they go easily to the far places of the world, and they often know ways, which they call "the black gates," over foreign frontiers. There are Gypsy trails across the world that no other people know how to follow. The Gypsy *patrins* (road signs) of stones and arranged twigs and leaves mark such places. The signs are similar to those used by the American Indians.

The continual rough weather of our second winter and spring in New York made it difficult for me to visit many people distances away. Also, with a big apartment to look after, and my children and dog, and no domestic help available, I always seemed short of time. Despite all the labor-saving devices to be found in towns, I always found that I had far less time than when living in primitive conditions in the countryside.

In New York there was endless dirt to wash away from the apartment – for I can never endure to be indoors for more than an hour without having the windows wide open, and the street dirt blew in upon us – and also to wash from my children's clothing and my own, and from the Afghan's shaggy coat.

Luz and Rafik and Gypsy friends; Granada

I would have liked to live like Diogenes in a barrel, to turn it around to face the sun, and to fill it with rain when I wanted to take a bath, and just to send it rolling down the road when I wanted to change my living place. I had a personal affection for Diogenes because of his rudeness to the conquering Alexander the Great, who, when impressed by Diogenes' bravery in refusing to flee from Athens with the other Greeks, deigned to stop and speak with him, but was told by Diogenes to get out of his way because his shadow was obstructing his sunbath! Alexander is said to have told his followers that one of the greatest benefits he had gained from his conquest of Greece was meeting with Diogenes and learning from him the importance of sunbathing, on which Diogenes had discoursed at length.

Or I would like a house like the American Indian poem:

House made of Dawn!
House made of Evening Light!
House made of Dark Cloud!
House made of Male Rain!
House made of Dark Mists!
House made of Female Rain!
House made of Pollen!

Getting meals in New York was simple. We lived mainly on pleasant-tasting New York bread, made to a formula by monks in a monastery outside New York; and we ate Indian succotash, the good yellow corn with beans; also "brinza," a ewe's milk cheese from Greece or other Balkan countries and sold in Greek, Rumanian, or other foreign shops; uncooked oat flakes; and all the natural greens we could find, such as parsley and dandelion, dill and fennel, which had usually been spared the poison sprays of the market gardeners of New York State because those plants were not liked by insect pests. Also nuts and fruits. Our fruits were limited because of the chemical spraying.

Greengrocers in New York were sarcastic about my search for fruit that was not speckled with the white powder of poison sprays: "Everything is done that way today," they told me. "Better not buy any fruit if you won't have the sprays." But I did not cease to search, and sometimes I found good things. I remember a find of tangerines in New York's Chinatown that looked as if they had arrived that very hour directly off some Chinese schooner, glowing bright and free from any vestige of chemical spray, and gathered in some natural orchard, those glowing tangerines, so fragrant and with their green leaves still fresh. I did not have much money with me on that visit to Chinatown, otherwise I would have bought every tangerine on that street-corner barrow. As it was we had to be content with a large bag holding five pounds of the delicious fruit – the best fruit we ever ate during all our time in New York.

We went many time to Chinatown in New York. We went the way past the impressive City Hall buildings and the Law Courts. Thousands of starlings come to those old buildings at every twilight to roost on window and other ledges, crowding together for warmth during the cold nights of New York's winter and early spring. And those multitudes of birds make more continuous discussion and noise than the lawyers themselves when the courts are in session. Hawks sometimes nest on the heights of New York skyscrapers and prey on the starlings and pigeons.

All who go to Chinatown for the first time, and for many more times, and who like the bizarre and the unusual, are fascinated. Especially if they have never been to the country of China – and we had never been there.

Chinatown is within walking distance of Greenwich Village, and we used to go there from the Village. Thousands of Chinese inhabit the locality of narrow streets and old houses. Many strange and picturesque things can be purchased there, even if they are often rather flimsy, and the quaint toys of nodding Chinese boys and girls or swords of the suicides adorned with bright silken tassels break in the children's hands before they reach home.

I liked the pharmacy shops where herbs were sold for use in old-fashioned herbal recipes, and in which shop tea from beautiful teapots was served free to clients. For sale in the various stores were kites shaped like butterflies and dragons, really too beautiful to send up into the sky for the winds to tear, and good enough to adorn the wall of any room. Writing brushes were offered, and paints that sparkled with silver when applied. Golden bells, wooden beads, and real dried sea-horses. The sea-horses were not only considered lucky but had use in medicine, being laid on fevered bodies to reduce fever. But being very fragile, they were easily broken and were therefore a costly treatment.

Much Chinese ginger was available, sugared or bottled in syrup. As both my children and I are lovers of ginger, we were very pleased to be able to buy so much that was so delicious and cheaper than one could find it anywhere else. Sugared ginger is an old sailor's remedy against seasickness. It is very effective – we always took it with us on our travels. The more that I used and learned about ginger, the more I valued it as one of the greatest medicines and foods, almost a cure-all, like the queen of all the herbs (and foods), garlic.

The festivals in Chinatown soon after the New Year were memorable: the lanterns at night, the first spring flowers. In the procession of dragons, great birds, wild animals, and a variety of legendary things of ancient China, it looked strange to see blue jeans and baseball shoes below those carnival-dressed bodies in the procession – the popular dress and footwear of the modern youth of New York's Chinatown.

In Chinatown so much pig grease (pork fat) was used in so many foods that eating out in restaurants was always difficult for us, being vegetarians, and anyway, very anti-pig. I was therefore pleased to learn from a friend who knew Chinatown well, that if one ordered the "Monk's dish," it would be purely vegetarian. This dish was prepared in China for the monks, who being often Buddhist are therefore vegetarians. [Some Buddhist monks, including the Dalai Lama, eat meat; they are not required to be vegetarian.]

Getting to and fro to places in New York was not easy. Although the streets are mostly laid out in a systematic plan, especially in Manhattan (Brooklyn was the most confusing to me of all the boroughs), I still got hopelessly lost. The formula for traveling in New York is: "be well-briefed before setting out, then ask questions of everyone when in need, including bus drivers, subway guards, postmen, policemen, and perfect strangers."

Once when I asked our direction from a "perfect stranger," I was taken far from where I wanted to be, and indeed found myself with my children in one of the most sordid parts of the Bowery, where there were open lots filled with rubbish and the earth was quite black with accumulated grime, where indeed it could be said that "filth shoved against filth," and where, even on a winter's day, because it was sunny that noon, tramps lay around on the ground, as an American writer has described them, "like dead bodies on a battlefield," around which one had to step with embarrassment, for the tramp bodies sprawling on the ground seemed either asleep or drunk. Although it was daylight, very large rats ran around, sometimes across the sleeping bodies. The sight of those terrible, menacing rodents made us tremble and we decided to hasten away before one of those rats bit us!

However, from that "direction-giver," seemingly a workman going home for his midday meal, I received a lesson on bus-riding with children in New York. "Never," he said, "pay bus fares for them until they are big enough to go into adult clothes or the boy's voice is breaking. If you go paying for youngsters like this, the bus guys will expect all us New Yorkers to pay for our kids, too. Few of us can afford that!"

"But," I informed the man, "my boy starts reading aloud all the advertisements in the buses. I tell him not to do it, but he persists."

"Oh, the driver's too busy to hear that," he consoled.

He told us untruthfully that our direction back to Greenwich Village was on the same bus that he was taking. When the bus came in he said to me, "Now don't be cowardly – remember, no fares for either of them!"

So I did not pay, and my boy read out all the ads as usual! I had learned a lesson, and I could use it on other travels when one does not have to show a passport. The world makes life so expensive for children everywhere, it is helpful to save a little sometimes.

It was often a relief to get into a taxi and cease to worry about finding one's way about, and the terrible roads to be crossed with two children and a large dog. Many times we were caught out in the center of the roads by the changing traffic lights. Then the traffic advanced relentlessly upon us, and people in the vehicles shouted at us, on either side, that we should not be there. The taxi drivers were the loudest and the angriest. At a mad speed, life on wheels passed by, and if we took a wrong step here or there, either one of us, one or all of our own lives would have been crushed out within seconds, like ants beneath advancing human boots.

I pitied the blind people in New York, with only their seeing-eye dogs to get them across the great New York avenues and streets. It was amazing to watch the dogs follow the light signals and then advance with their owners into the streets. All the blind women that I saw wore red hats, though that may have been coincidence, red hats being popular then in New York. A friend had given me one for a Christmas present. I know that in the woods of Maine red hats are worn by people as a warning to the hunters not to shoot in the direction of the wearers, a precaution made necessary by the big number of human beings shot there instead of birds and animals.

I heard of one red-hatted blind woman, with empty slits in her face where eyes should have been, saying to her boxer dog whom she had felt move when the traffic lights turned green: "Jump to it, Skipper, get me across before fear gets me." Woman and dog stepped into the roadway, safe for so few minutes between the lights. Nor were the roads ever really safe, because traffic can come around corners, legally, when the lights are red, and so run one down. [This is no longer the case in Manhattan.]

Death on the New York streets meant the funeral parlors, with their smart facades and perpetual lamps lit. Such places frightened me, and I always hurried past them. Dead, I would rather lie in state like the old Gypsy Queen on Henry Street, as described in this book, with my friends comforting me – not put away in storage in some refrigerated place. I do not like modern funeral arrangements.

I hope when I die it will be in some primitive place where my soul, before it finally departs from all association with the body, can be comforted with candles and flowers (especially rosemary), and tears and disorder. A canvas sheet weighted with heavy stones and taken far out to sea would be my most favored burial, however.

My children and I had agreed: if death on the roads, no funeral parlors for any of us; we would insist – by refusing to pay for them!

It was an escape from the crossing of streets on foot when one rode in taxis, but often it was impossible to get a taxi in New York. They all swept by filled with passengers.

At certain hours of the day, the lunch hour around twelve to one, the evening end-of-work hour around five to seven, and the theater hour a little later – one could cry in vain for a taxi. Also, even an empty taxi will not always stop for a fare. They just pass one by. Once I asked a taxi-driver about this: Did the taxis pass by the poor and seek those who looked richest?

He said that that was not so, that sometimes they would not stop because of the crowding traffic making a change of direction difficult, or they really did not see or hear, or did not want to take children, and so on. In the main, drivers preferred the poor because they usually tipped better! He had often picked up a rich party coming out of one of New York's best restaurants where they had spent possibly many hundreds of dollars between them, and they would tip him a dime! In New York, taxi-drivers – as a matter of law – write down descriptions of any fares that look irregular as they step into the cab.

An alternative to taxis in New York is the subway. This runs beneath the city in a colossal spider web pattern and has replaced the former – noisier and dirtier – elevated

Central park: Rafik, Luz, and the dogs, Leila and Jaroon.

railways and streetcars in New York City. Sometimes, when I had to get to appointments and knew that I would not be able to find an empty taxi at that time, I had to face the ordeal of the New York subway during rush hour. That was always an incredible experience – there is nothing like it in any other city where there is underground travel, and I have been in most of those cities.

The thousands of commuters who live outside New York and travel to and from the city daily, often by subway as the quickest means of transport, have to suffer daily the horrible experience of being treated as sardines. The New York subway cars during rush hours have been called "mechanized sardine cans." Only at least those fish are so packed in that they do not fall out of the cans, whereas the subway passengers who have the misfortune to be packed near the automatic doors of the cars are pushed out onto the platform at almost every stop, and then have to fight to get back in again.

Arms and legs get caught in the closing automatic doors; there is rarely an injury to anyone because the doors are not weighty, but clothes can be torn. Subway travel during rush hour is a game of "push and shove."

Riding the subway one winter from Astor Place in the Village, going towards Pelham Park, I was unable to avoid the rush hour, having an appointment to keep. After five minutes of slow suffocation, and recalling all the while the descriptions of the packed death trains taking the Nazi victims – Jews and Gypsies – to the gas chambers, I decided to leave the train station before I had reached my destination. Grouped around me had been five foreign-looking men, all wearing strange, very tiny, dark trilby hats. Each lurch of the train brought blasts of the men's breaths to me. They had seemingly been eating heavily of garlic and chocolate, and the mixture was sickening to smell. One could not help but think of gas chambers.

The always unpleasant air of the subway platform seemed sweet and balmy to me after the suffocating human breath-packed air of the subway car. I stood on the platform for a while, taking my time. I had missed my appointment now and need not travel farther for the time being. I thought about the better scents to be found in New York, of the springtime flower shops with their massed violets and hyacinths, and of the hot fragrance coming from the many bakeries that make their own bread. I watched loaded train after loaded train go by. Every car of every train was crammed with suffering passengers.

I marveled at what people could endure in the name of progress. Although the Gypsies of New York and most places in America now largely travel by automobile – cars and trucks – they have things to say about modern travel. They seldom go by plane. They say that in a car or a train, on foot or on a horse, one stands a chance if misfortune comes, but on a plane one will be lucky if any pieces can be found for burial afterwards, if the plane fails.

People in New York were still talking about the collision of two planes over Brooklyn. It had made unbearable reading in the newspapers: one little boy was tossed from one of the planes into the snow on the street and found – well enough for his rejoicing parents to believe that they would be able to keep him with them on earth. But, internally, his lungs had been burned, and he died close to Christmas.

Almost as terrible to me as the crash of the planes was the loss of the twenty-eight men on the radar tower, which was swept by winter storms into the Atlantic Ocean, seventy miles southeast of New York City. The stark horror of being trapped under the sea with enough air to make survival possible for a while. Because, as with the Gypsies who love so much their *bavlow* (the wind), an abundance of air is always so necessary to me, I vowed that never in my life would I be in a subway rush hour again!

One interest of subway travel is to study the faces of the people, and the great variety of hats that they wear. I think that more varied hats are worn by men and women in New York than in other cities that I know. I especially remember the strange hats of winter, in all kinds of furs and all colors of wool. Men as well as women wore bright winter hats. Some women sewed big sequins of glittering silver and gold onto their woolen hats, which flashed in the dim subway light. One African-American woman wore a black woolen hat low down on her forehead, with no hair showing. In the front of the hat, low on her brow, was sewn a huge rose made of yellow chiffon. That yellow rose against her mascara-black skin was beautiful indeed!

Friends of mine used to buy many hats and other things from the thrift shops. I think there are no shops like those in any other city. The shops deal in secondhand clothes and other things, and in many cases the profits go to charities. America being a prosperous nation, fine hats and dresses and coats find their way into those shops, sent by rich people who do not like to appear in front of their friends wearing the same clothes more than a few times!

I used to take my children to look at the thrift shops. It was fun to see city clerks preening themselves in front of mirrors while they tried on velvet smoking jackets and velvet caps with tassels of gold. Matrons trying on revealing chiffon evening gowns and funny unsuitable hats that they would never consider from an ordinary shop, but in the thrift shops, everything was at such bargain prices, and one never knew what one would find there, from fine furs to good snow boots. One shopped, prepared to be daring! One might even find a bridal gown. An unmarried friend, Bettina, bought one from a Manhattan thrift shop, and when I last saw her, she was seriously considering going to a marriage bureau to find herself a husband, so that she could wear that glamorous bridal dress.

When the winter weather turned subzero, New Yorkers did all sorts of things to themselves. As protection against the cold, both men and women wore pads over their ears, attached to elastic around their heads [earmuffs]. They stuck pieces of white fluffy cotton, what the English call cotton wool, onto their cheeks with adhesive tape to avoid frost chapping. They wore woolen mufflers covering their mouths and just allowing the nose to breathe. Women friends of mine put on two and three skirts to keep their legs warm, if they were not wearing the popular woolen trousers of many colors.

I think I only suffered once in New York's cold when driving from Manhattan to Sands Point, Long Island, with my friend Cynthia Madigan. The trouble was one of New York's strikes. The trains were not running, and therefore there were thousands more commuter cars on the roads than usual. And there was a near blizzard blowing. The weather was below zero. The journey to Long Island, which normally takes far less than an hour, lengthened into over three hours. It all seemed to me like a fantastic dream. The rows upon rows of waiting cars, like trapped beetles unable to move. The piled snow turned all colors by car lights and street lamps. The noise of impatient auto horns. The cold, which truly froze one's blood. We passed cars that had broken down on the snow ridges that had cut open their tires. Our progress was slower than an earthworm's, but at least we moved at times. To be held up completely in the snow, in that blanket of cold, must have been an ordeal that I hope never to have to suffer.

When I was visiting Cynthia's home on Long Island, enjoying the fun of her charming children and her tame birds and pack of dogs, Irish Wolfhounds, Salukis, and my favorite breed, Afghan hounds, the evening drive from Manhattan to the Sands Point part of Long Island was very pleasant. I loved seeing so much light reflected on so much water. Sometimes the evening sky at dusk made its own light, in yellow rainbeams striping the surrounding gray.

So much water around New York! With its unique hundreds of miles of waterfront, and, in many parts in the city environs, old taverns or new bars where roving bands of foreign sailors gathered, most of the men interesting in appearance and speech. I sometimes took my children to the waterfront places to see the sailors ashore, playing card games with the excitable noise that Gypsies make at cards, or playing dice games, making music on the traditional mouth-organs, kissing the blowsy barmaids.

My children enjoyed speaking Spanish again with the many Spanish-speaking sailors that we met from such places as South America, Mexico, and even some from Spain itself.

Among all the crowding foreigners that one sees in the New York streets and the city environs, all the time that I was in the city and so much in its streets, I only twice saw Gypsies walking there. In Paris, Istanbul, Athens, and all the towns of Spain, one sees the Gypsies frequently, whereas in London and New York, the Gypsies are rarely seen, although they are numerous in both cities.

The first time that I saw Gypsies out in a New York street was in Brooklyn, near where the great Brooklyn Bridge crosses the East River. The Gypsies were a group of five women, and they were in Gypsy dress, the bright-colored headscarves and the long-skirted dresses, narrow at the waist and filled and wide at the hem in the shape of bell-flowers. Only they wore drab-colored winter overcoats that covered most of their bright dresses. They were on their way to distemper [a painting process] apartments, and they carried with them clanging buckets, some empty, some filled with colored distempers, green and pink and blue, of various shades. In their hands they also held brushes with long handles, with which to apply the distemper to clients' apartments. I spoke with them; they told me that they were from Rumania, but had been living in America for years.

The second time was on Third Avenue. I saw a middle-aged Gypsy woman out on a cold winter's day, with only a fringed scarf over a blouse of thin-looking material. Her skirt was showy and also unusual wear for a winter's day with snow lying deep on the sidewalk, where it had newly fallen. It was of royal blue satin with silver strands like spiders' webs. I saw her go into a shoe shop and was tempted to follow her because she was a Gypsy and therefore interested me. So I too went into the shop to try on footwear that I did not intend to purchase.

I watched the Gypsy make a selection from many pairs of slippers. Hers was a powerful yet harsh face, and I did not want to talk to her. She chose a pair of bright red leather slippers with stilt heels. They looked very costly – possibly the best pair of slippers in the shop. I could see no others that equaled them.

When the Gypsy told the shop people to keep the goods for her and that she would be back soon with the money, and then left the premises without leaving any money as deposit on her choice, I asked the shop people if they really would keep the slippers for the Gypsy. They told me that they would, that Gypsies often came to the shop, which they seemingly recommended one to another, and that they always came for things when they promised to do so; they seldom brought money with them on their first visits.

I noticed that the Gypsy in the blue skirt, true to the usual way of her people, did not carry a purse. Gypsy women keep their money either against their breast, where a tight waistband of skirt or dress helps to hold the money secure – they rarely wear brassieres or corsets, finding it uncomfortable to restrict their body freedom in any way (and I share their way of dressing) – or they carry money pinned to their clothes, usually inside their skirts.

Before leaving New York I went around to most of the Gypsy families that I knew, leaving with them dolls and other things my children had been given for Christmas that were too many and too bulky to take with us on our new forthcoming far travels. Their favorite toys, to which several had been added during our stay in America and Mexico, both lands of fabulous toys, were allowed to travel with us.

The Gypsies said that they would watch for our return to New York, and they foretold that we would be back there again before the passing of many years.

If my children had had their choice, they would not have been leaving New York at all! It is said of New York children that the major physical activities of most of them are climbing into a bus, opening the refrigerator, and turning the television dial. Yet my children had been happy and active there and had kept healthy.

I had had to spend nearly seventy dollars on bottled spring water during our winter and spring stay in that city, as I could not allow either my children or dog, nor I myself, to drink of the water that fumed with chlorine as it came from the tap. We drank spring water, sold in very large glass flasks, delivered to our apartment direct from the spring. Water is a human lifeline, and I have always taken care that our supply should be clean and natural.

The children had played ball games around the blocks with other children, and the snow games learned and played were things they would be remembering with pleasure for years after, indeed forever.

I too had been happy and well-entertained in the city. But despite the allure of New York, who would choose to spend the springtime in any city, away from real contact with nature and the marvelous stirring of the life forces of the earth that come with every spring? None of this can be felt and enjoyed along streets of concrete, and in apartment houses out of all contact with the natural soil and its trees and flowers, animals and birds. One caught a glimpse of spring's coming in Central Park, but that was merely tantalizing. I wanted the full and unrestricted pleasure of spring and summer and autumn for every year of my life – only winter would I sacrifice to town living.

I felt with that Gypsy lad from the Buchenwald concentration camp, mentioned earlier in this book, who called to the other nervous prisoners by the camp gates: "What are you waiting for? Come along with me. I am a Gypsy and glad to be out here in the open air where the birds sing. It's good to belong to the countryside."

I am a Gypsy, and it is good!

We had farewells to say to friends who worked at the United Nations. I was always happy to be in that vast place, for people of all colors of skin and all religions walked its premises secure from slights and insults. Self-confidence could be seen on the faces of all peoples there. One felt that the words of President Kennedy in one of his many really splendid speeches were truthful when he said, concerning the United Nations, that there "any nation can exert influence, not according to the strength of its armies but according to the strength of its ideas."

On my farewell visit to the United Nations, a group of Russians were playing chess by clock, which compelled quick moves. I was sorry that I had never seen the leisurely chess being played on the big outdoor chessboards of red and black stone, on one side of Washington Square in the village. There the masters played the old, slow chess, surrounded by their admirers.

Rafik and I sat and watched, from a distance, the excitable and yet grimly concentrated chess play of the Russians. Then before I could stop him, Rafik had left me and seated himself among the chess players.

I felt that nothing could be more annoying to the Russians than to have an inquisitive strange boy among them disturbing their concentration. Therefore I called to Rafik to return to me. But one of the Russians put his arm around the boy and said, "It's okay with me, honey-bunch, you can stay around."

Such cinema American coming from his mouth in his un-American face was amusing and also lovable.

Rafik stayed, and a Japanese man with the Russian group, Russian-speaking himself, explained to him – in English – the details of the play.

Later Rafik was persuaded by his friend Jess Aland, in her office, to dance Gypsy flamenco for a group of admiring secretaries gathered there. It seemed strange to hear the quick and wild stamping of the Gypsy dancing among the quiet and the severity of the United Nations building.

Before, and on, our day of departure from New York, my children were laden with gifts from neighbors and shopkeepers who had known us. Fortunately the gifts were mostly candy and comics, which could be used up during the journey and therefore would not further burden our luggage. Mimi, Rafik's Hungarian "lady-friend" who kept the kiosk on Second Avenue near 79th Street, from whom he used to buy comics and drawing books, presented the little boy with gifts of both, and also lollipops for Luz. The kindness of New York shop people, and their interest in our well-being and in our travels, will not be forgotten.

Only once did my children get into trouble in a New York store. It was on First Avenue, and in their enthusiasm for toys they knocked over a pyramid display of dolls, which all tumbled to the floor! By good chance none were broken, and there was no damage to pay, but both children were quickly put outside the shop and told emphatically not to return.

Our sailing day from the Port of New York was a day of light – of that bright winter and spring New York sunlight that Jan Yoors told me inspires all the artists who work in that city. And New York, as we drove through it on our way to the big American Export Line's liner, was beautiful. More beautiful than I ever remember seeing it. Now two days of warm spring sun had driven away the lingering, blackened snow. There were yellow-green tips showing on the dark filigree of the few New York trees that we passed, and birds twittered from trees and roofs. I lingered in the city looking at trees and listening to the birds and enjoying the sun-gilded beauty of pigeons as they sunned themselves or sped across patches of sky held between the towering buildings of Manhattan. I was mindful of Madame Prince and her pigeons.

To each his own, and those were my interests: the sun, the trees, the birds and the Gypsies.

As I say in *Traveler's Joy*:

> You shall die, and I shall die!
> Take our places in sky.
> You and she, and he and I,
> When the time comes, all must die.
> That's a game we would play,
> Man and woman, girl and lad,
> In Gypsy camps far away,
> Laughing timid, yet passing sad.
> We would shout King Death to come,
> Laughing loudly, turn and run.
>
> Gone the Gypsies everyone,
> All who played the Gypsy game,
> Left the earth, its mirth and fun,
> Starry nights and hyacinth lane.
> None can play that game alone,
> Thus I want to hear the cry,
> Come now leave thy earthly home,
> Join the Gypsies in the sky.

We were late at the port, almost the last passengers to embark on the liner then ready for departure. I was reprimanded for such lateness. Gypsies have no sense of time! Overmuch they stand and stare, to look at little things. We had entered New York as Gypsies and we were leaving unchanged in our ways, but richer in experience of life and of the Gypsy race, and richer in friends; and we had come to know another city.

Also in New York I had found new markets for the books that I had written and would write in the future. Therefore a useful time, providing financial help in a world of very cruelly increasing prices.

Now we were leaving for the Middle East, for continuing wanderings, and again to fulfill my longing for the quiet places of the earth, for contact with unpaved, natural territory, for the pleasure of unhampered sunlight and moonlight away from the tall buildings, for winds untainted by factory fumes. And for meetings with wild animals and birds, and to hear their voices, their songs, and to see and touch flowers, and herbs, and trees, that no man had planted nor trimmed nor sprayed with poisonous chemicals. All that was very urgent in my body and soul.

So goodbye to New York, the Big Apple! I thank you deeply, for I saw and learned much. I will not forget!

> On a necklace around your throat, you wear the cross,
>   Gypsy woman!
> And in your arms, the burdens of the ages
> And in your smiles, pain of thorns
> And in your heart, wounds of wars.
> But in your soul are the rays of light, peace and
>   goodwill.

For Juliette; from Jose Cordosa de Sousa,
Isla de Flores, Azores, Portugal

Copyright Notice

Acknowledgments

For the current edition, © 2011

A Gypsy wink and a big basket of thanks to the wise women who made this book a reality:

- **Jane Bond** and **Kimberly Eve** for turning Juliette's words into electrons.
- **Kimberly Eve** for her wonderful cover illustrations, interior illustrations, and design skills
- **Jennifer Jo Stevens** for seeing to the never-ending details: the quotes, the numbers, the codes, the facts.
- **Betsy Grace Sandlin**, best friend of words and guardian of the commas.
- **Rose Weissman**, for diligent, delightful assistance.
- **Rev. Ursula Carrie Wilkerson** for scanning photos.
- **Andrea Dworkin** for design assistance.
- **Susun Weed**, for typesetting, editing, designing, and keeping it all humming along.
- Our **guardians**, **grandmothers**, **spirit sisters**, and the **Ancient Ones**.

Susun S. Weed (left), editor-in-chief of Ash Tree Publishing, shamanic herbalist, goatkeeper, and lover of women, is thrilled to have this chance to bring Juliette's words and wisdom to the current generation of herbalists.

Kimberly Eve (right) is head of the art department and chief artist at Ash Tree Publishing. She has worked to bring several of Juliette's books back into print.

Juliette de Bairacli Levy (1911–2009) is honored as the grandmother of modern American herbalism. She has devoted her life to the health and well being of domesticated animals, especially dogs. Her herbals and memoirs have been in print, and in use, for over fifty years.

Other books you will want to read from

Ash Tree Publishing

Women's Health, Women's Spirituality

Wise Woman Herbal Series

best-sellers by

Susun S Weed

Wise Woman Herbal for the Childbearing Year $11.95
Healing Wise, Everyone's Herbal $17.95
New Menopausal Years, The Wise Woman Way $16.95
Breast Cancer? Breast Health! The Wise Woman Way $21.95
Down There, The Wise Woman Way $29.95

Herbals of Our Foremothers Series

classics by

Juliette de Bairacli Levy

Nature's Children $11.95
Common Herbs for Natural Health $11.95
Traveler's Joy $11.95
Spanish Mountain Life $16.95
Summer in Galilee $24.95
A Gypsy in New York $21.95

and, by **Maida Silverman**

A City Herbal $13.95

To order:

- Visit www.wisewomanbookshop.com
- Write to PO Box 64, Woodstock, NY 12498

Prices subject to change.